Felting
The Complete Guide

Jane Davis

cincinnati, ohio
mycraftivity.com
connect. create. explore.

Felting The Complete Guide. Copyright © 2009 by Jane Davis. Manufactured in China. All rights reserved. The patterns and drawings in this book are for the personal use of the reader. By permission of the author and publisher, they may be either hand-traced or photocopied to make single copies, but under no circumstances may they be resold or republished. It is permissible for the purchaser to make the projects contained herein and sell them at fairs, bazaars and craft shows. No other part of this book may be reproduced in any form or by any electronic or mechanical means including information storage and retrieval systems without permission in writing from the publisher, except by a reviewer who may quote brief passages in a review. Published by Krause Publications, an imprint of F+W Media, Inc., 4700 East Galbraith Road, Cincinnati, Ohio, 45236. (800) 289-0963. First Edition.

media

Other fine Krause Publications craft books are available from your local bookstore, craft supply store or direct from the publisher at www.fwmedia.com.

13   12   11   10   09   5   4   3   2   1

Library of Congress Cataloging in Publication Data
Davis, Jane
  Felting : the complete guide / Jane Davis.
    p. cm.
  Includes index.
  ISBN 978-0-89689-590-4 (alk. paper)
  1. Felt work. 2. Felting. I. Title.
  TT849.5.D38 2008
  746'.0463--dc22

DISTRIBUTED IN CANADA BY FRASER DIRECT
100 Armstrong Avenue
Georgetown, ON, Canada L7G 5S4
Tel: (905) 877-4411

DISTRIBUTED IN THE U.K. AND EUROPE BY DAVID & CHARLES
Brunel House, Newton Abbot, Devon, TQ12 4PU, England
Tel: (+44) 1626 323200, Fax: (+44) 1626 323319
Email: postmaster@davidandcharles.co.uk

DISTRIBUTED IN AUSTRALIA BY CAPRICORN LINK
P.O. Box 704, S. Windsor NSW, 2756 Australia
Tel: (02) 4577-3555

Editor: Jennifer Claydon
Designer: Michelle Thompson
Production coordinator: Matt Wagner
Photographers: Jane Davis and Tim Grondin

ACKNOWLEDGMENTS

With each book I've worked on over the years, many people have contributed to the process along the way, some in direct ways, and others in more subtle ways. I'd like to thank the many people who have helped to get this book completed.

Many thanks to Candy Wiza, for seeing that covering the many aspects of felting could make a great book. Thank you to my wonderful editor, Jennifer Claydon, for the deadlines that always help so much in getting a book to print, and for your patience in me getting the material to you. Thank you to the art department for your beautiful work on this layout and all the wonderful project photos that I didn't have to take. Thanks to Jonathan for being my hand model, so I could take the how-to photos.

Thank you to my students whom I learn from as much as they learn from me. Thank you to Lois Varga of Anacapa Fine Yarns in Ventura, California, for your encouragement with my teaching and getting me to *finally* set up a Web page.

And as always, thank you to my family, Rich, Jeff, Andrew and Jonathan. You complain, but you live with it, and there's an opening in this pile where I can still get through to climb out from under the yarn—at least once in a while.

Contents

Introduction

The first time you witness loose fibers felting together is an extraordinary experience. Knit or crochet a big, floppy bag or hat, then throw it in the wash and watch it magically transform into a fuzzy, dense creation. You can arrange fibers and agitate them with hot soapy water to mat them together into a wonderful new material. There's also needle felting—my new passion—which is painting and sculpture wrapped up with the fabulous texture and color of wool.

It never ceases to amaze me that people have discovered so many fascinating uses for animal hair. The more I explore felting, the more artists and craftspeople I find who are experimenting to create new arts and crafts never seen before. However, these expansions on the art of felting start with a craft that is as old as the domestication of sheep.

Today, felt is all around us, and not just in crafts. From dampers on piano keys to washers in car parts, you can find felt in surprising places. And most felt products today are still made from sheep's wool.

This book is about all things felting. We'll begin with a general felting overview, including basic processes, materials, tools and terms. Over the next several chapters, different felting techniques will be covered in detail, starting with techniques and ending with a variety of projects using the featured technique. Then, we'll combine several techniques into a variety of projects to show how the techniques can be used together.

I hope the projects and techniques in this book will inspire you to strike out on your own felt adventures. Have fun and go felt something!

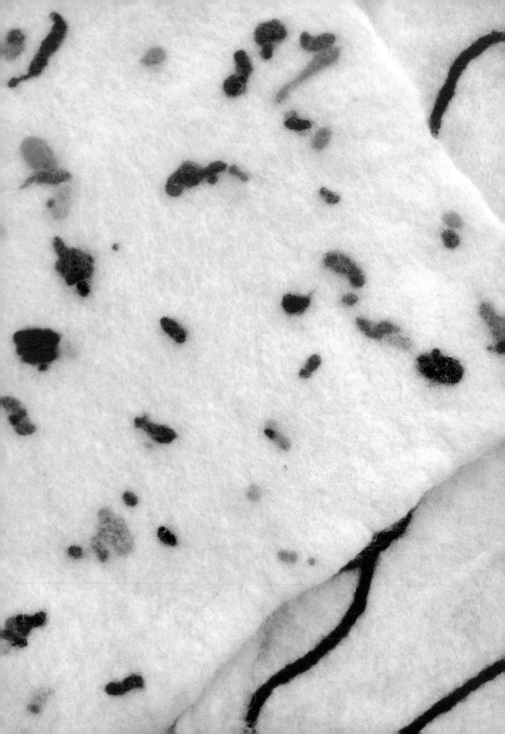

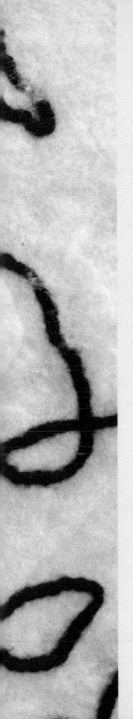

Felting Basics

This overview will introduce you to the tools and materials used in felting and to the many different methods used to felt. For more detailed information on each felting technique, be sure to see the following chapters. There you will find step-by-step instructions, as well as beautiful projects, that will help you expand your felting knowledge.

What is Felting?

The actual process of felting is simply the tangling together of animal fibers and locking them together permanently. This process takes place because of the unique characteristics of wool fibers, which have scales covering their surface. The scales relax when warmed, opening away from the shaft of the wool fiber. If fibers tangle together while the scales are open, they will lock together permanently when the scales close back down to the shaft.

The felting process can happen in several ways. Over time, fibers that are constantly rubbed through day-to-day usage can felt together; this often happens to wool sweaters, especially at the underarms, where there is a lot of movement. A combination of heat, moisture and friction is the quickest way to make felting occur. Fibers can also be forced to lock together without heat or moisture by using barbed needles, called felting needles, to cause friction between fibers.

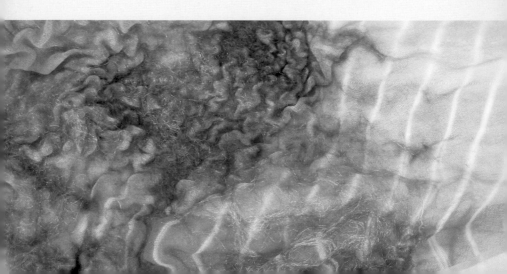

Fiber, Yarn and Fabric

There aren't many supplies needed to create felt. The most basic materials are animal fibers and a tool to agitate and tangle the fibers. However, talented felt artists have come up with many creative new ways to felt, including combining animal fibers with fabric, yarn and other materials. These emerging ideas open up a host of possibilities for felters to be even more creative. The following materials can be used alone or in combination as the base of your felted creations.

Fiber

Almost any animal fiber can be used to create felt. Some types of animal fiber will felt more easily than others, although the method used to felt will also affect how fast felting occurs. A good rule of thumb is that the finer the fiber, the more quickly it will felt. The most common ways to measure wool are thickness (micron count) and by a calculation of the number of yards of yarn that can be spun from a pound of wool (spinning count or Bradford count). Most wool sold for felting is a merino blend that is 24 to 28 microns, which is equal to a Bradford count of 56 to 60; this is the type of wool used for all of the projects in this book. However, there are many other fibers available to felters; make sure to have fun and experiment!

Wool for felting is widely available in three forms: worsted preparation, woolen preparation and locks. In a worsted preparation, the fibers have been combed so that short fibers are removed and the remaining fibers lie parallel to each other. Crossing worsted fibers over each other in different directions during felting helps the fibers tangle together more easily.

In woolen preparation, the fibers have been carded instead of combed and retain the shorter fibers. This fiber preparation felts easily because of the mingling of the short fibers with the long fibers. Woolen preparation is ideal for needle felting because the fibers mat together quickly from the needling action. However, it can be difficult to achieve smooth, clean lines in a design because of the short fibers.

The last form of fiber that is commonly used in felting is locks. Locks are often used as accents in abstract art, or as hair for figures or animals. The wool for locks is carefully cut and washed so that the locks remain intact, without being altered.

A SAMPLING OF WOOL FIBERS

From left to right: worsted merino, woolen merino cross blend, Lincoln/Romney, Shetland, Cotswold, Leicester Longwool, Longwool locks

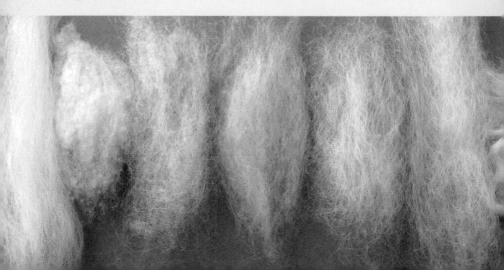

In addition to natural colors, fibers for felting are available in a rainbow of dyed colors. Dyed fiber samplers provide a fabulous palette for creative work with felt. You can purchase several different samplers and blend the colors for unlimited color possibilities.

A dyed fiber sampler

Felting kits are another product available to crafters; from needle felting to wet felting, a growing number of products provide the essentials to try out a project or technique. Kits can be very convenient because you can try a technique without worrying about choosing the right supplies. Many kits provide instructions in addition to tools and materials.

A great time saver for felt artists is prefelt, a sheet of wool fibers that are lightly felted together in a fragile fabric. Prefelt can still felt to other fibers, making it a great material to cut into shapes and then felt to other fibers

A felting kit

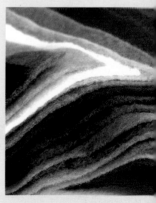

Prefelt in a variety of colors

Single-ply yarns felt well and also work well with needle felting without showing a lot of the needle holes.

These two-ply yarns felt easily, though the plies show needle holes from needle felting more than a single-ply yarn would.

Yarn

Yarn is composed of fibers that have been twisted, or spun, together into a continuous strand. In order to felt, a yarn must be composed of at least thirty percent feltable wool. Don't choose washable yarns for felting projects; they have been treated with a coating that keeps the tiny scales from locking together.

Yarn can be a wonderful addition to felt projects. Yarn can be wet felted by hand, or a washing machine can be used to full yarn after it is woven, knitted or crocheted. For a dimensional effect, needle felt yarn onto felted items or fabric. Yarn can also be sandwiched between layers of fiber for an interesting effect in laminated felting.

Fabric

Any fabric that wool fibers can migrate through can be used in felting. Loosely woven fabrics make the process much quicker and easier, and fabrics that contain feltable wool are an even better choice because a stronger bond will be formed with the felted embellishments. However, you can successfully felt through fine fabrics that have no wool content at all.

A scarf blank is a great base for a felting project. Since the fabric is already hemmed, you only have to felt it and then you have a beautiful finished item.

Scarf blanks for felting projects

Tools

The tools you need for a felting project will depend on the technique you plan to use and whether you are using loose fibers or yarn. Needle felting requires few tools and no water. A knitted or crocheted item can be thrown in the washer, and therefore requires few tools. However, you may find that you will end up combining techniques when you felt, so it is good to have a reference of all the items you might need. Following are the tools you will need to use for every technique throughout the book.

Bamboo mats are used for wet felting by hand. The project is rolled up in the mat, then the coiled mat is rolled back and forth to create friction to felt the fibers together. A sushi mat works well for small items, and a bamboo shade like the one shown is great for a large item.

Beading supplies, such as beads, needles and thread, are sometimes used to embellish felt projects. Containers to hold beads when working and to store beads when not in use are also handy.

Bubble wrap can be used instead of a bamboo mat for wet felting by hand. Use bubble wrap with bubbles that are ¼"–½" (6mm–13mm) wide. Blue pool-cover bubble wrap is best for repeated use because it is sturdier than packing bubble wrap.

Crochet supplies include crochet hooks, scissors, removable stitch markers and tapestry needles. To complete the crochet projects in this book, you will need these tools as well as a knowledge of basic crochet techniques.

A dowel rod or foam pool noodle can be used to help roll up a project for flat or rolled felting. The rod you use should be at least as wide as the project, mat or bubble wrap. A dowel rod can also be used directly on the surface of a project to harden the item.

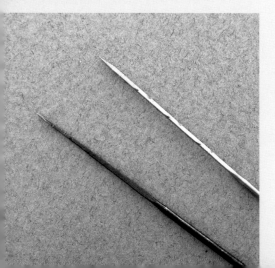

Felting needles are triangular- or diamond-shafted needles that have small barbs along their length. They are used to force fibers to tangle together, creating felt. Felting needles come in several sizes, from coarse (size 36) to fine (size 42).

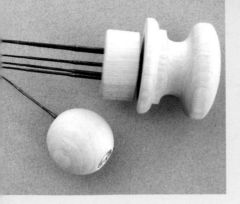

Felting needle holders are real hand savers! There is a wide variety of holders available for felting needles—work with the one that is most comfortable for you. Needle holders can hold a single needle for detail work, or several needles for larger areas.

Hand carders are brushes that can be used to blend and align yarns and fibers. Hand carders look like extra-large dog brushes and come in sets of two.

Hat-making supplies make creating a hat much easier and more accurate for sizing and specific hat shapes. Hat forms, stabilizing ribbon, decorative ribbon and hat stiffeners, such as water-based shellac, will help create a professional-looking hat that holds its shape.

Knitting supplies such as knitting needles, scissors, stitch markers and tapestry needles are used to complete the knitting projects in this book. You will also need a knowledge of basic knitting techniques for the projects.

Measuring tools are indispensable to the accuracy of a project. A scale comes in handy for weighing materials. A measuring tape is used to measure projects in progress. And occasionally you will need a calculator to work out sizing for garments or other items.

A needle felting mat should be used under needle felting projects to protect you and your work surface. Felting mats can be foam or large flat brushes, or any surface that has give, but doesn't snag on the felting needles too much.

Pounding tools are used to create a firm finish on felted items. Steaming and pounding felt compresses and firms it. Any hard item will work, but I have found that wooden kitchen tools, such as meat tenderizers, are perfect for the job.

Soap diluted in water helps fibers slide easily together during the felting process. I prefer Ultra Ivory Dishwashing Liquid, but you can use any soap you choose.

Steam helps greatly to compress felted items. You can press felt with a steam iron to get crisp edges and a flat surface, or use an iron to form felt into its finished shape. You can also use the steam from a tea kettle to warm and wet felt before forming it into its finished shape.

Sticks, from toothpicks to dowel rods, are helpful tools for creating circular shapes in felting. Loose fibers can be wound around sticks into coils for use in needle felting.

Additional Items

In addition to the tools I've already mentioned, there are a few more things that you might want to keep on hand; they aren't necessities, but can be very helpful. Towels are useful for soaking up extra soapy water during hand felting. Plastic trash bags can serve many purposes, such as protecting a work surface or acting as a barrier between sections of a piece so that they don't felt together. Rubber bands can be used to hold rolled work together during felting. Straight pins and clothes pins can be used to hold your work in place and for shaping.

Terms

The processes and materials used for felting have specific terms that are helpful to know when you are working from written instructions. Many of these distinctions are casually interchanged, but each has its own specific meaning.

A batt is a sheet of fibers that have been carded on a drum carder. A batt is usually about 1"–2" (3cm–5cm) thick and 12" (30cm) wide and comes rolled up in a cylinder.

Blocking is the process of shaping a finished felted or fulled item into its final form before drying. The blocking process for felt is more aggressive than for knitted or crocheted items because felted items are forced to assume shapes they would never take on their own. Once the felt is the desired shape, it must be allowed to dry completely. Sometimes a stiffener is added to help the felt hold its shape.

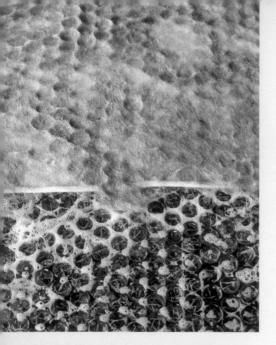

Fulling and felting are terms that are often used interchangeably, but they have different meanings. Felting is the process of matting loose fibers together into a solid fabric. Fulling is the shrinking process that takes place after the fibers are intertwined. For example, a knitted bag can only be fulled, not felted, since it is already a fabric. This distinction is rarely made in felting conversations, since it is a fine distinction.

Hardening is when the fulling process is continued until the felted fabric is firm and dense. There are many degrees of felting. Once a piece is felted enough so that the fibers are tangled together, you can stop there and have a finished item. However, in some cases, you will want a firm material and will continue the process by hardening the piece.

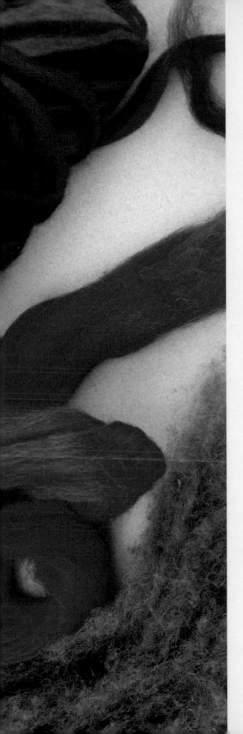

Rolag, roving, sliver and top are terms that are often used interchangeably to refer to fibers that have been cleaned and either carded or combed, and are ready to use for spinning or felting.

A rolag is a loose rope of fiber several inches thick in which the fibers have been rolled off a carder or carding machine so that they are jumbled together in the rope. The fibers are in a woolen configuration rather than parallel as in sliver, top or roving.

Roving is a loose continuous rope of fiber approximately 1½"–2" (4cm–5cm) thick. The fibers in roving have been pulled off a carding machine so that they are aligned in the rope. This is the common term used for most fiber sold for felting. The fibers are aligned and in a worsted configuration. Pencil roving is the same as roving except that it is approximately ½" (1cm) thick. Sliver is a thinner rope of roving.

Top is roving which has been further processed and combed, removing the fibers less than 3" (8cm) long, leaving the remaining fibers more aligned than the other forms of fiber described. This is the final worsted form of fiber.

Felting Methods

Even though the end result of every felting process is locked and matted fibers, there are many paths to get to that end result. Time and friction will cause felting slowly but surely, and felt artists and craftspeople have found many ways to speed up the felting and fulling processes. The following overview of varying felting procedures defines the basics of these processes.

Hand felting can be used as a general term for all forms of felting other than the machine method, but the term also refers to a specific process. To hand felt, simply wet fibers or a knitted, crocheted or woven item in warm, soapy water and rub until the fibers felt, without the use of bubble wrap or a bamboo mat.

Throwing is a method used to harden a felted item. This is done in wet felting when the fibers have matted together but are not completely shrunken. Throwing is done by actually dropping a project or slapping it against a hard surface, such as a table.

Steaming and pounding are used mostly for traditional felt hat making. Hat makers begin with a generic bell-shaped, partially felted blank, then thoroughly steam, pound, pull and shape the felt around a hat form.

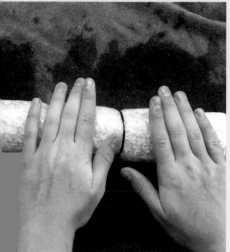

Flat felting, or rolled felting, is a technique that has been used to make felt for hundreds of years. This process starts with laying the item to be felted on a sheet of bubble wrap or a bamboo mat. You then wet the item with warm, soapy water and use a stiff rod to roll up the item in the mat or bubble wrap. Next, you secure the roll with rubber bands and roll, roll, roll, usually fifty to one hundred times. Then you unroll the project, rearrange it on the mat or bubble wrap, add more soapy water and roll again. Continuing in this manner creates a felted item. There are several variations and additional steps depending on the actual project, but those are the basics. The process allows much more control over the felting than machine felting; however, there is still some uncertainty, since shifting can happen when the fibers are rolled up into the mat.

Laminated, or Nuno, felting is the addition of fabric to the flat felting process. The felting fibers are adhered to a loosely woven or feltable wool or wool-blend fabric. You can also add other elements during the felting process, such as metallic thread.

Needle felting, or dry felting, is done with a special barbed needle. Fibers can be felted together by poking the needle into the mass of fibers repeatedly until they tangle and mat.

Machine fulling is used to full knitted, crocheted or woven items, or to further full fibers that are felted enough to stand up to machine agitation. The item is placed in a top-loading washing machine on the lowest water level with a bit of soap on the hot wash/cold rinse setting and left to agitate in the machine until it is fulled as desired.

Tips for Success

You can take steps to control the felting process, but it is not an exact science. Projects can often turn out much differently than you may have originally intended. Usually this is a result of not being able to see what's going on, such as when felting in the washing machine or when rolling a bundle of fiber. Here are some simple tips to help make every felting experience successful.

— First and foremost, always try to keep an open mind about a project. A piece may not turn out as intended, but if you let the piece evolve, you might be surprised with a new idea that is just as beautiful, yet completely different from what it was "supposed" to be.

— When flat felting, be sure to check the progress of the felting and fulling often to see how far the felting has progressed, and to check that your design hasn't shifted. Any changes you want to make to a design when flat felting need to be done fairly early in the felting process so that the moved fibers will felt to the surrounding fibers.

— Needle felting can correct many mishaps created in flat felting, including filling in unwanted holes, thickening thin areas of felting and, of course, adding a decorative touch to a plain felted item.

— If you have two sections of felt that you wanted to adhere to each other and they didn't, you can try placing a small tuft of fiber between them and felting them again. If this doesn't work, try needle felting.

— If you are not successful in your first felting attempt, you can sometimes re-wet and further felt your piece to correct the error or create a different project.

— It is always a good idea to wear gloves when working with felt, especially if you have sensitive hands or are worried about them drying out.

CHAPTER TWO

Wet Felting

Felting loose fibers is a versatile technique that can be used to produce many different creations, from simple objects like the Easy Ball *on page 52, to beautiful accessories like the* Shaped Lady's Hat *on page 76 and the* Nuno Scarf *on page 94. The degree to which the fibers are felted and the technique used for felting are both important parts of the process. These are creative as well as practical decisions that you will need to consider while developing a project.*

The Basics of Wet Felting

The following three processes are the basic requirements for wet felting. Many techniques can be added to these basic steps to create different effects in your finished pieces.

Wetting the Fibers

The first step when wet felting is to fully saturate the fibers with warm, soapy water. Covering the arranged fibers with nylon mesh helps the fibers stay in place as water is sprinkled or sprayed on the fibers. After wetting, the wet fibers are patted down by hand. This process compacts the layers of wool so that you can see how thin or thick the layers are. At this stage, the fibers haven't meshed together at all, so more fibers can be added if you see that more are needed.

Agitating the Fibers

The next step, agitation, causes the fibers to tangle together. The type of agitation varies depending on the felting method used. The warm, soapy water relaxes the scales on the surfaces of the fibers. While the scales are open, the fibers are tangled together. As the water cools, the scales try to close back down to the fiber shaft, locking the tangled fibers together. This is the key to felting. Depending on several variables, this part of the process can take a very short time, or a project may require a lot of agitation to finish. You can continue felting and fulling a project until it will go no smaller or tighter and is as dense as it will go, or you can stop the felting process earlier so that the fabric is soft and drapeable.

Shaping the Finished Project

After a project has felted as much as it should for the desired effect, it will need to be formed into its finished shape. This might be as simple as lightly steaming to even the edges, or it might mean pushing, pulling and pinning to the shape you want, then letting the project dry completely. Some pieces will also require a stiffener, such as the water-based shellac used in hat making.

Additional Felting Factors and Techniques

It's easy to felt something: Just throw a nonwashable wool sweater in the washer and dryer and see what happens. It shrinks down several sizes and gets thick and fuzzy. What's not always easy is controlling the process so that you get your desired results. And working with loose fibers that can slide around means you need to follow a few basic steps before the fibers have locked in place. Following are some of the many techniques and surface treatments that you can use to achieve different effects in felting, with a step-by-step description of the basic process and tips to help you on your way.

Degrees of Felting

Fibers can be felted together to different degrees, from slightly matted together to felted, fulled and shrunk down so tightly that they become stiff, strong and very dense. At times, you will want your fibers to be one or the other of these extremes, and often, you will want something in between. All of the different degrees of felting have a purpose and a use. It's important to monitor where your fibers are in the felting process so you can know when felting is complete, and know how to get to the next level.

Uniformity

If you take three handfuls of fiber that you think are about the same amount, roll one into a loose ball, one into a tight ball and leave one loose, you can see that it is difficult to measure amounts of wool without a scale. You can try to estimate fiber amounts, but once you begin to do a lot of felting, you will find that a scale comes in handy. Weighing the fibers to get the correct amount is more reliable than estimating. If you want to make the same item several times, or if you are laying out fiber over a large area, you will want to weigh the wool to make sure you have the same amount in each section.

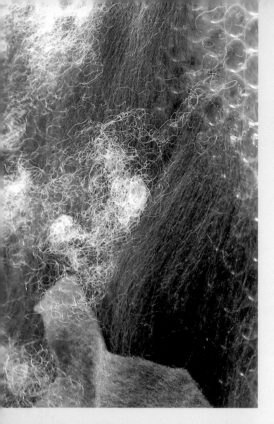

Shading

Beautiful effects can be achieved in felting by using different colors of fiber to create shading. Try using several different colors overlapped slightly to create a color progression on your piece. Using small wisps of fiber will make subtle color changes, while using large, thick sections of fiber will make strong color changes. Using colors that have a strong contrast, such as black and white, creates a bolder image.

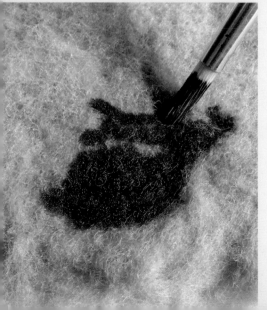

Dyes

Dyeing adds one more dimension to the design process. Many types of dyes can be used directly on fibers during felting to produce a unique piece in the colors of your choice.

Adding Dimension

To give dimension to a project, different elements of the piece can be felted separately, then added to the piece so that they won't felt to the rest of the fibers. This creates a section that will stick out from the main body of the project. One method for adding dimension is to create spikes by rolling a length of fiber between your hands until it compresses. The felted portion of the spike is then wrapped in plastic, leaving an unfelted tail of fiber to felt to the body of the project.

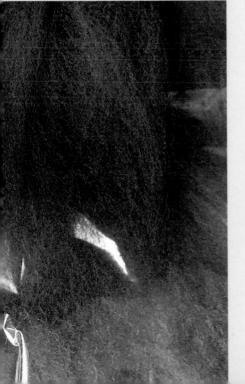

Resists

Another method that can be used to give dimension to a piece is to use a resist. Placing a piece of plastic between layers of fibers creates a place where fibers can't felt together, resulting in separate layers of felt. This can be used in many ways, such as to make graduated layers on a scarf, or to create a pocket in a bag.

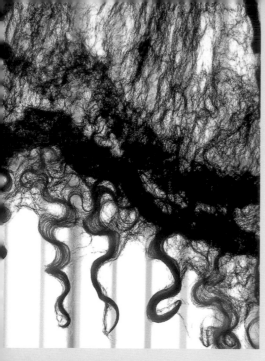

Cobweb Effects

Cobweb felting is loosely defined as a light, open mesh of fibers that have been felted together. It is characterized by openings in the finished item, from large holes to airy meshes. Making cobweb felt can be tricky because when working with smaller amounts of fiber you need to be careful to check every step of the process so that you don't get holes where you don't want them. A common problem felters encounter when creating a cobweb piece is that too little fiber is laid out for the original design and the piece needs to be re-felted to fill in gaps.

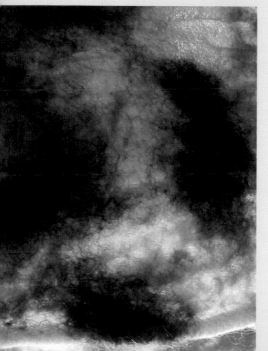

Laminated, or Nuno, Felting

Laminated, or Nuno, felting is a felting technique that combines fabric with fiber. A fabric that is loosely woven easily allows fiber to migrate through the weave so that when the piece is felted, the fabric is shaped by the contracting fibers creating a unique texture while strengthening the overall piece.

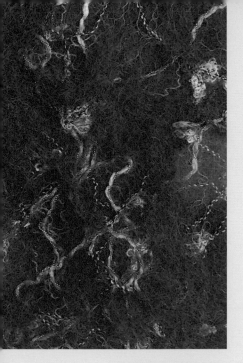

Adding Materials and Yarn

Another great embellishment to wet felting is a layer of items such as yarn or small pieces of fabric joined to the piece by a very thin layer of fiber. This embeds the added items into the surface of the felt, creating unique texture and color in the finished piece.

Combining Techniques

Wet felting combines very well with other felting techniques, as well as with many other crafts. Needle-felted embellishments make a great addition to a wet-felted project. Sheets of felt can be cut and sewn like other fabrics to create new projects. See Chapter Five for projects that use multiple felting techniques, or stretch your creativity and see what combinations you can come up with.

MATERIALS

- 4 oz. (113g) feltable wool fiber
- 12" × 12" (30cm × 30cm) or larger piece of bubble wrap
- Netting (optional)
- Hot, soapy water in a spray bottle or shaker
- Dowel rod
- Rubberbands
- Cool water for rinsing
- Dry towel
- Steam iron (optional)

Flat Felting, Step by Step

Following are the basic steps you will need to follow to create flat felt projects using the rolling technique with bubble wrap. For this example, I used 4 oz. (113g) of wool, creating an approximately 7" × 7" (18cm × 18cm) piece of felt. Try using this technique to make test samples of new fibers or when you want to experiment with embedding items in felt. The resulting squares can be used to create a variety of items, from quilt squares to Christmas ornaments.

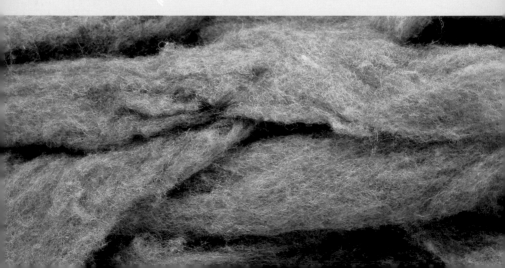

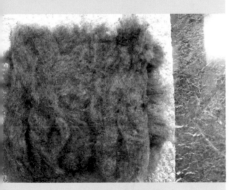

1 Laying out the fibers

Lay out fibers parallel to each other on a sheet of bubble wrap. To make a 7" × 7" (18cm × 18cm) piece of felt, cover at least a 10" × 10" (25cm × 25cm) area with the fibers at least 1" (3cm) thick. Lay out a second layer of fiber on top of the first, with the fibers of the second layer aligned perpendicular to the first. Repeat the process 1–2 times more, so that you have 3–4 layers of fiber stacked up, each perpendicular to the previous layer.

Tip

Fibers will felt as long as they cross each other, and some friction, warmth and water are applied. However, many felters have rules about the direction that the fibers need to be laid out for the best felting results. Experiment with different methods to find what works best for you, but here is one suggestion on how the fibers can be laid out. Because the fiber is cut, there is a wider cut end and a thinner, pointed end. If you lay the fibers so that the cut ends face all four points of the compass, the felt will be more even. This means you will need to make four layers, laying each layer in a different direction.

2 Wetting the fiber

Using a spray bottle or a water bottle with multiple holes in the lid, sprinkle hot, soapy water over the surface of the wool. Pat down the wool so it is fully saturated. Some felters like to get their hands soapy so the fibers won't stick, and others like to cover the surface with netting before adding the water. Use the method that works best for you.

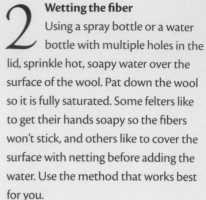

3 Rolling and securing

Using a dowel, begin to roll up the bubble wrap and fiber. Adjust the fibers as you work so that they don't wrinkle or fold as you tightly roll everything around the dowel. Secure the rolled bundle with rubber bands.

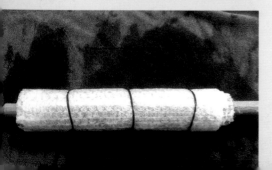

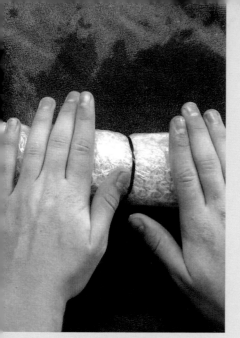

4 First rolling

Roll the bundle back and forth on your work surface around 50 times. You can make short rolls with just your hands, adjusting the bundle every few rolls so you are working each part of the bundle, or you can make long rolls, rolling from the tips of your fingers to your elbows so that you are sure to cover all sides of the bundle with each roll. If you make short rolls you will need to work longer than if you make long rolls.

5 Check progress

After approximately 50 rolls, carefully unwrap the bundle and check the progress of the felting. You should be able to lift the piece and rotate it so that you can roll it up from a different direction. Look to see if there are any unwanted holes or weak areas in the piece, and fill them with more fiber. This is the last chance to add new fiber before the fibers start sticking together too much to add more fiber.

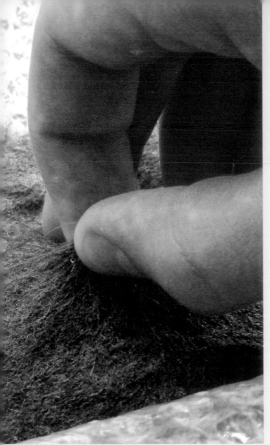

6 Continue rolling

Add more warm, soapy water, then repeat Steps 3–4. Check the progress of the felting again. Use the pinch test to see if the fibers have felted.

To perform the pinch test, pinch a little bit of the fiber and pull on it lightly to see if the fibers are beginning to stick together, creating a felted skin. If the fibers pull apart easily, they are not yet felted, and you have more rolling to do. If the fibers stick together, you can begin to handle the project a little less gingerly—the piece can be picked up and moved more easily. Be careful to pinch in an area that won't be affected much if the fibers move a little, since you may pull the fibers apart if they have not felted yet. It's best to do the pinch test away from decorative elements, such as a prefelt design or specialty fibers that have been carefully placed.

7 Rinsing

Repeat Steps 3–6 until you are satisfied with the degree of felting. Once the piece is felted, remove it from the bubble wrap and rinse it in cool water. Squeeze out as much extra water as possible.

8 Hardening (optional)

If you are satisfied with the texture of the piece of felt, move to the next step to finish the piece. If you want the fabric to shrink more and/or become firmer and stiffer, you can harden the felt.

To harden the felt piece, roll it around the dowel without bubble wrap and roll it again, applying pressure. Unroll and reposition the piece and roll it again. Repeat this in all directions until you are satisfied with the texture of the felt.

9 Final shaping

Roll the finished piece of felt in a dry towel to remove as much water as possible. Lay the piece flat or shape as desired. Let the piece of felt dry completely.

To make a very firm, flat piece of felt, steam press the damp felt instead of laying it flat and allowing it to air dry.

Dimensional Felting

Making Balls and Dimensional Objects

Balls of felt can be used for anything from toy balls to jewelry components. Making a ball of felt sounds like an easy process, but the correct technique must be used to make a ball of felt that doesn't have folds or wrinkles in the finished piece. To make a firm 1" (3cm) ball, use approximately 2g of fiber. Roll the fiber into a tight ball and needle felt the end in place (see *The Basics of Needle Felting*, page 104). Needle felt all over the piece to form a tight, smooth-surfaced ball. Wet the ball in warm, soapy water, then roll it between your palms until it begins to hold together and become more dense. Continue to roll the ball between your palms, passing it under very warm running water, or dunking it into a bowl of warm to hot water to wash out the soap and further felt the piece. When the ball is the desired size, roll it in a towel to get out as much moisture as possible. Let the ball dry completely. To make the surface less fuzzy, roll the finished ball under an iron set to the cotton setting with steam.

Working Over a Mold

To make hollow balls or shapes, such as bowls and hats, you can felt over a form, such as a ball or wooden egg. Beth Beede, a well-known feltmaker, developed and taught a ball felting technique that is the basis for this process. The first step is to cover the form with fiber in three or more layers, each layer perpendicular to the previous one. Then, carefully wrap the fiber-covered form with nylon hose or some other elastic fabric, and tie the ends closed. Finally, wet the whole piece with warm, soapy water and massage the surface until the fibers are felted. Once the fibers have condensed and felted a bit, you can also gently bounce the ball by dropping it on a hard surface—but don't be too rough; you don't need to play basketball with it! As you work, you will need to unwrap the fabric cover several times to check the progress of the felting. When the piece is fully felted, remove the fabric cover, cut a hole in the felt and pull out the form. You can make hats, bags, balls, trumpet-type flowers and many other hollow forms with this method.

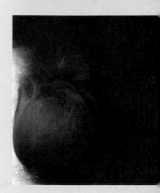

Working Flat then Stuffing

Another technique that can be used to create dimensional shapes is to make a hollow piece of felt by flat felting, then stuff the piece of felt.

To do this, you will need a flat pattern for the item that is made out of a material that can get wet, such as plastic. Working on bubble wrap, lay out several layers of fiber perpendicular to each other, covering an area approximately 1" (3cm) larger than the pattern in all directions. Wet the fibers with warm, soapy water and place the pattern on top of them. Fold the fibers that extend beyond the edges over the pattern, then cover the pattern with more layers of fiber. Wet the added fibers and smooth the excess to the other side of the piece.

Roll the fibers, along with the bubble wrap, around a dowel rod. Secure the bundle and felt, checking often to make sure that the entire pattern is covered evenly with fiber (see *Flat Felting, Step by Step*, pages 42-47). When the fibers are felted, rinse the piece, then cut an opening in the felt large enough to remove the pattern. Remove the pattern from the felt, form the piece and allow the felt to dry. Stuff the piece with nonfelting fiber fill, and sew the opening shut. Needle felt over the opening if desired to further hide the seam.

Tips for Success

— A common beginner's mistake is to lay down too little fiber when flat felting. Dry fiber has so much more volume than wet fiber, so it looks like there is a lot more fiber than there actually is. When the fibers are wetted, you will see holes in the surface if there is not enough fiber. When you lay down several layers in different directions you can usually avoid this, but it's always good to keep in mind how much your pile of fibers will shrink and add a little more.

— When adding nonfelting elements to a project, such as small pieces of fabric, you should first lay down several layers of fiber, then add the nonfelting elements. Top this with a very thin layer of feltable fiber, just enough so that the nonfelting elements are covered but still visible. When this stack is felted, the thin layer of fibers will act like a net to hold the nonfelting elements in place.

— If your wetted bundle of fibers is cold, you can warm the fibers up again by holding a steam iron over the fibers. Hold the iron about 12" (30cm) over the work and steam the area, then roll that section up and steam the next area. Be careful not to hold the iron too close or you may melt the bubble wrap or damage your work surface. Warming the whole piece will help the fibers to full more quickly.

— When the fibers are laid out, ready to be dampened, you can wet them evenly without using a net by spraying the water over the top of the fibers rather than directly on the fibers. The mist will fall like a gentle rain.

Easy Ball

With this project you get the chance to try both needle felting and wet felting without a big investment in time or materials. This is a great way to try out felting to see what it's all about. This project uses surface felting to create a soft ball that is light and bouncy. The soft shape is achieved by felting only the surface fibers and leaving the fibers on the interior of the ball unfelted.

The project shown at left was made using Harrisville Designs Fleece in the following colors: 002 Red, 011 Emerald, 067 Marigold and 030 Azure.

SKILL LEVEL
Beginner

FINISHED SIZE
Diameter: Approx.
2½" (6cm)

MATERIALS
2 oz. (57g) feltable
  wool fiber
Small amounts of
  feltable wool fiber in
  3 contrasting colors
Size 36 felting needle
Felting mat
Warm, soapy water
Cool water for rinsing

1 Prepare the ball

Roll the main fiber into a tight ball and use the felting needle and mat to condense the fiber into a smooth ball shape that has no folds or creases (see *Dimensional Felting*, page 48). If needed, use small tufts of fiber to cover folds in the forming shape. Do not felt the fibers completely.

2 Begin embellishments

When you are satisfied with the shape of the ball, use the other colors of fiber to make spirals or other shapes on the surface of the ball, tacking them in place with small jabs of a felting needle. The ball should be fairly tight and almost the finished size.

3 Felt the ball

Get your hands wet and soapy in warm, soapy water. Rub the surface of the ball, being careful not to compress it. Don't dunk the ball in water. The ball should be wet on the surface, but not soaking wet all the way through. Roll the ball in your hands without much pressure until the surface of the ball is matted and the fibers don't pull apart. Rinse the ball in cool water to remove all of the soap. Allow the felt to dry completely.

Beaded Bauble

This project is a fun, easy ball beautifully embellished with beads. It's a great way to practice making uniform felt balls. Even if the baubles don't come out perfectly uniform you may find, if you add a few beads to them, you can make a beautiful creation just the same. Unlike the *Easy Ball* on page 52, you do need to get all of the fibers in this ball wet so that the fibers are condensed throughout the piece, creating a firm, tight ball. Balls like this are great to embellish with beads or embroidery. They can also be shaped into forms other than spheres.

The projects shown at left were made using Harrisville Designs Fleece in colors 031 Cobalt and 008 Hemlock.

SKILL LEVEL
Beginner

FINISHED SIZE
Diameter: Approx. 1"
 (3cm)

MATERIALS
2g feltable wool fiber

Size 36 felting needle

Felting mat

Warm, soapy water

Cool water for rinsing

Iron and ironing
 board

Approximately 125
 size 11 seed beads

Beading needle

Beading thread to
 match wool color

1 Preparing the ball

Roll the fiber into a very tight ball and use the felting needle and mat to condense the fiber into a smooth ball shape that has no folds or creases (see *Dimensional Felting*, page 48). If needed, use small tufts of fiber to cover folds in the forming shape. The ball should be fairly tight and almost the finished size, like the center ball shown in the picutre below.

2 Felting

Soak the ball in warm, soapy water until the water penetrates all of the fibers. Roll the ball between your palms; start with gentle pressure, then increase pressure as you feel the fibers becoming firm and compacted, until you are rolling firmly on a tight ball. Continue felting until the ball is dense and firm. Rinse the ball in cool water to remove all of the soap. Use an iron set to the steam setting and roll the ball between the iron and the ironing board for a few seconds so that the fibers flatten against the ball. Allow the felt to dry completely.

3 Beading

Thread a needle with a 20" (51cm) strand of beading thread and take a ¼" (6mm) long stitch into the felt ball. Pull the thread almost all the way through, then make a small back stitch, and pass the needle through the loop before pulling the stitch tight. Cut the tail thread close to the ball.

String 1–3 beads and take a stitch in the felt ball, coming out of the ball where you want the next stitch to begin. Continue attaching beads in this manner until you have a pattern of beads around the ball. Experiment with different stitch designs, such as spirals or wavy lines.

Beaded Tassel

This design shows how useful felt is for beading. Because you can stitch into it anywhere on the ball, you can use a felted form as a base for any type of beadwork, from minimal to ornate. The felted ball can be completely covered in beads, used as a form for the beadwork or it can be a part of the finished design surface.

The project shown at left was made using Harrisville Designs Fleece color 008 Hemlock.

SKILL LEVEL
Beginner

FINISHED SIZE
Diameter: Approx.
 ¾" (2cm)
Length: Approx.
 3¼" (8cm)

MATERIALS
2g feltable wool fiber

Size 36 felting needle

Felting mat

Warm, soapy water

Cool water for rinsing

Iron and ironing
 board

281 size 11 seed beads

77 size 8 seed beads

12 4mm round beads

11 6mm faceted
 crystal beads

10 10mm dagger
 beads

2 teardrop beads

2 20mm trumpet
 flower beads

1 8mm faceted crystal
 bead

Beading needle

Beading thread to
 match wool color

1 Preparing the ball

Roll the fiber into a very tight ball and use the felting needle and mat to condense the fiber into a smooth ball shape that has no folds or creases (see *Dimensional Felting*, page 48). If needed, use small tufts of fiber to cover folds in the forming shape. The ball should be fairly tight and almost the finished size.

2 Felting

Soak the ball in warm, soapy water until the water penetrates all of the fibers. Roll the ball between your palms; start with gentle pressure, then increase pressure as you feel the fibers becoming firm and compacted, until you are rolling firmly on a tight ball. Continue felting until the ball is dense and firm. Rinse the ball in cool water to remove all of the soap. Use an iron set to the steam setting and roll the ball between the iron and the ironing board for a few seconds so that the fibers flatten against the ball. Allow the felt to dry completely.

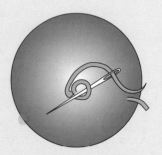

3 Begin beading

Thread a needle with a 20" (51cm) strand of beading thread and take a ¼" (6mm) long stitch into the felt ball. Pull the thread almost all the way through, then make a small back stitch, and pass the needle through the loop before pulling the stitch tight. Cut the tail thread close to the ball.

FIG. 1   FIG. 2   FIG. 3

4 Continue beading

String the beads as shown in Figures 1–3. Take a stitch into the felt ball at the top of each pattern repeat, approximately ³⁄₁₆" (5mm) away from the previous repeat. Repeat the beading pattern 10 times, creating a circle of beads around the top of the ball. Anchor the thread to the felt ball with small back stitches, then bring the thread out at the center top of the ball.

To create the loop for hanging the tassel, string 15 size 11 seed beads on the beading thread, then take a small stitch in the ball. Pass the beading thread through the loop beads and the ball several times to make the loop strong.

5 Finish beading

Pass the beading thread through the ball to the center bottom of the ball and string the dangle as shown in the picture at left. Make several small back stitches in the ball and cut the thread close to the ball.

Christmas Cookie Ornament

This little cookie with frosting and sprinkle embellishments is just the thing to add to a Christmas tree. Although this project can be made using commercial felt, it's much more cookie-like with thick, handmade felt. A detail like this is one reason to make your own felt, rather than use commercial felt. When you make your own felt, you can customize it to your needs.

The project shown at left was made using Harrisville Designs Fleece in the following colors: 044 White (A) and 042 Camel (B); and DMC size 5 pearl cotton in the following colors: 726 Light Topaz, 946 Medium Burnt Orange, 798 Dark Delft Blue, 422 Light Hazelnut Brown and Ecru.

SKILL LEVEL

Beginner

FINISHED SIZE

Approx. 4" × 4"
(10cm × 10cm)

MATERIALS

4 oz. (113g)
feltable wool fiber
in 2 colors (A and B),
2 oz. (57g) each

Bubble wrap

Netting (optional)

Warm, soapy water

Dowel rod

Rubberbands

Cool water for rinsing

Dry towel

Steam iron (optional)

Freezer paper

Scissors

Size 5 pearl cotton in
assorted colors

Sewing needle

1

Make felt

Make 2 5" × 5" (13cm × 13cm) pieces of felt, one in a "cookie" color (B) and one in an "icing" color (A) (see *Flat Felting, Step by Step*, pages 42–47).

2

Transfer the pattern

Copy the cookie pattern below onto a piece of freezer paper; cut out the 2 star shapes. Iron the smaller, wavy shape to the "icing" felt and the larger star to the "cookie" felt. Trim both felt pieces to match the pattern, then remove the freezer paper.

Pattern shown at actual size.

3 Embroider sprinkles

Thread a 20" (51cm) length of pearl cotton on a sewing needle. Embroider the "icing" felt star with ¼" (6mm) long straight stitches to resemble sprinkles, leaving room to add stitches in other colors.

Repeat with additional colors of pearl cotton.

4 Sew layers together

Place the embroidered "icing" felt on top of the "cookie" felt. Thread a length of pearl cotton to match the "icing" felt on a sewing needle. Begin embroidering around the edge of the "icing" felt using a blanket stitch (see diagram below), being careful to stitch into the "cookie" felt, but not all the way through. Blanket stitch around the edge of the "cookie" felt with matching pearl cotton, as well. Make a small loop with the thread for hanging. Weave in the thread ends.

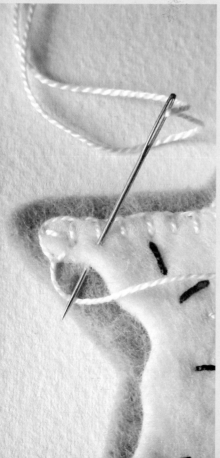

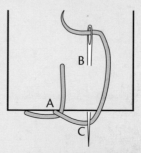

Easy First Scarf

This easy scarf is fun to make because you get to play with fibers and yarn and just see what happens. Because it doesn't matter how straight your edges are, or how thick your finished piece is, you can have fun experimenting with the materials and learning about what happens during felting.

The project shown at left was made using Harrisville Designs Fleece color 002 Red; 1 ball S. Charles Ritratto (53% viscose, 28% kid mohair, 10% nylon, 9% polyester, 1¾ oz./50g, 198 yd./180m), color #73; 1 ball Tahki Pansy (100% nylon, .9oz/25g, 163 yd./150m) color #02; and 1 spool Coats 40 wt. Rayon thread, color #135C.

SKILL LEVEL
Beginner

FINISHED SIZE
Approximately
8" × 48"
(20cm × 122cm)

MATERIALS
4 oz. (113g) feltable wool fiber

1 (1¾ oz./50g, 198 yd./180m) skein of metallic yarn

1 (.9oz/25g, 163 yd./150m) skein of nylon yarn

1 spool rayon thread

Bubble wrap

Netting (optional)

Warm, soapy water

Dowel rod

Rubberbands

Cool water for rinsing

Dry towel

Steam iron (optional)

1 Laying out the fibers

Lay out a layer of wool fibers on the bubble wrap, parallel to the length of the scarf, covering a 9" × 50" (23cm × 127cm) area. Taper the ends of the scarf.

Add a 2nd layer of fibers perpendicular to the 1st layer.

Lay a 3rd layer parallel to the first layer.

Layer the yarns and thread on the fiber in swirls and loops over the full surface of the fibers.

Lay a last layer of fibers over the yarns and thread to cover them, but keep it thin enough that the yarn is still visible.

2 Felting the scarf

Felt the scarf (see *Flat Felting, Step by Step*, pages 42–47). While felting the scarf, occasionally unroll the bundle and check to see that the fibers are evenly distributed and that the yarn is covered by fiber, with no more than 1" (3cm) lengths of yarn exposed. Add more fiber where needed and continue felting. Gently push the ends of the fibers in along the sides of the scarf to create smooth edges on the scarf. This scarf can have wavy, uneven edges, but don't let the edges be thin. Use a steam iron to heat the fibers while felting. Continue to check the progress, steam and reroll the scarf until it holds together. Once you can lift the scarf from the bubble wrap without the fibers pulling apart, take the scarf off of the bubble wrap and place it in a sink or tub. Add soap and hot water and gently knead the scarf to further full the fibers. Once the piece is fulled to the degree you desire, rinse it in cool water and press out extra moisture with a clean, dry towel. Steam press the finished scarf if desired and allow the felt to dry completely.

Storm at Sea Scarf

This delicate and airy scarf reminds me of the ocean, from the wavy prefelt pattern to the frothy seashore fringe. Making this cobweb project is not too difficult as long as you are careful to check your work early. Make sure that there is enough fiber to hold the scarf together, but not so much fiber that you won't have a transparent finished fabric.

The project shown at left was made using white longwool locks, Medium Grade Jeweltone wool in Ocean Blue and medium blue and dark blue prefelt sheets.

SKILL LEVEL

Intermediate

FINISHED SIZE

Approx. 7" × 75"
  (18cm × 191cm)

MATERIALS

2 oz. (57g) feltable
  wool fiber

1 oz. (28g) uncarded
  longwool locks

2 8½" × 11"
  (22cm × 28cm)
  sheets of prefelt in
  2 colors

Bubble wrap

Netting (optional)

Warm, soapy water

Dowel rod

Rubberbands

Cool water for rinsing

Dry towel

Steam iron (optional)

1 Cut prefelt

Enlarge the pattern below as directed and cut the pattern into pieces along the pattern lines. Pin the white pattern pieces to a lighter sheet of prefelt and the shaded pattern pieces to a darker sheet of prefelt. Cut the prefelt sheets following the pattern pieces.

Enlarge pattern by 200% to bring to full size.

2 Begin laying out fibers

Lay out the wool fibers on top of the bubble wrap in a diagonal direction; use light tufts that almost obscure the bubble wrap. Lay the prefelt shapes in rows near the ends of the scarf, alternating the lighter and darker pieces.

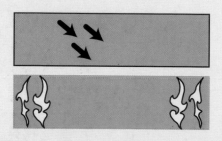

3 Finish arranging fibers

Arrange 8 or 9 longwool curls along each end of the scarf so that they overlap the wool fibers about 1" (3cm). Add some of the wool fiber horizontally over the portion of the curls that overlaps the first layer of wool fiber. Add small bits of the longwool curls across the surface of the scarf, like wave caps on a rough sea. Space the additional curls about 2"–3" (5cm–8cm) apart, covering the whole scarf.

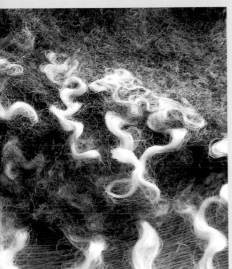

4 Felt the scarf

Felt the scarf (see *Flat Felting, Step by Step*, pages 42–47). While felting the scarf, occasionally unroll the bundle and check to see that the fibers are not too sparse and that the prefelt pieces haven't become folded or scrunched. Add more fiber where needed. Gently push the ends of the fibers in along the sides of the scarf to form smooth edges on the scarf. Use a steam iron to heat the fibers while felting. Continue to check the progress, steam and reroll the scarf until it holds together well. Rinse gently in cool water and press out extra moisture with a clean, dry towel. Steam press the body of the finished scarf, but not the locks at the ends of the scarf. Allow the scarf to dry completely.

Shaped Lady's Hat

The finished shape of this hat was determined by the bowl I used to shape the fibers. A large, shallow bowl will result in larger folds in the finished hat. A tall, narrow bowl will result in a hat that is fitted more closely to the head with less room for adding structural folds. Try this project as an experiment in felting to either mimic the hat shown, or branch out with your own unique creation.

The project shown at left was made using Harrisville Designs Fleece color 008 Hemlock.

SKILL LEVEL
Beginner

FINISHED SIZE
Circumference:
Approx. 22" (56cm)
at brim

MATERIALS
4 oz. (113g) feltable
wool fiber

Bubble wrap

Netting (optional)

Warm, soapy water

Dowel rod

Rubberbands

Cool water for rinsing

Dry towel

Steam iron

Large, round-
bottomed bowl

Rounded hat form
or head form

Clothespins

Water-based hat
stiffener

Ribbon flowers
(optional)

Sewing needle

Sewing thread to
match wool color

1 Laying out fibers

Lay out a layer of wool fibers, forming a circle with a 20" (51cm) diameter. Add 3 more layers of wool, each perpendicular to the previous layer.

2 Felting

Felt the wool fibers until they just hold together (see *Flat Felting, Step by Step*, pages 42–47). If the fibers felt too much, they will not easily form into a hat shape. Once the fibers are stable enough to lift off the bubble wrap, move the felt circle to the overturned bowl. Pat the felt down, forming it to the shape of the bowl. Add more warm, soapy water to the felt; rub and pat the surface of the fiber until it begins to hold together firmly.

Remove the felt from the bowl, fold it in half and roll it up with the dowel. Roll the dowel approximately 25 times. Unroll the felt, then fold it again in a different direction and roll it around the dowel so that you are rolling at a different angle. Repeat this several times until you have rolled the felt in every direction. The hat will shrink as you are felting it. When the fibers have felted completely, rinse gently in cool water and press out extra moisture with a clean, dry towel. Center the piece of felt on the hat form or head form.

3 Shaping

Pin curved creases around the top of the hat, creating a flowing design. Begin with a major curve from the back to the front of the hat. The first pleat runs along the side of the head, pulling in a deeper fold at the front and the back to help shape the hat so it fits the head. Next, make a second, smaller pleat next to the first and pin both pleats in place. Allow the pinned hat to dry completely.

4 Finishing

Remove the clothespins from the hat and steam press out any marks made by the clothespins. Trim away excess felt as desired to form a brim. Steam press the edges of the felt if needed to smooth out the brim. Wet the inside of the hat with hat stiffener. Make any desired changes to the shape of the hat and let it dry again on the hat or head form. Tack the folds at the front and back of the hat with sewing thread to hold the folds in place. Attach ribbon flowers if desired.

Cross-Section Posy

This lovely felted flower and leaf can be used as decorations on a bag, pin cushion or even as a fancy eraser for a white board or chalk board. These posies look great in a variety of colors, so be sure to try your favorite, or even work up a whole rainbow of posies!

The project shown at left was made using Harrisville Designs Fleece in the following colors: 067 Marigold mixed 1:2 with 011 Emerald (A); 010 Spruce (B); 009 Evergreen (C); 002 Red (D); and 021 Violet (E).

SKILL LEVEL

Intermediate

FINISHED SIZE

Flower: Approx. 2¾" (7cm) diameter

Leaf: Approx. 5¼" × 2¾" (13cm × 7cm)

MATERIALS

10 oz. (283g) feltable wool fiber in 5 colors (A, B, C, D and E), 2 oz. (57g) each

Sushi mat

Warm, soapy water

Rubberbands

Cool water for rinsing

Dry towel

Sharp knife

Size 36 felting needle (optional)

Felting mat (optional)

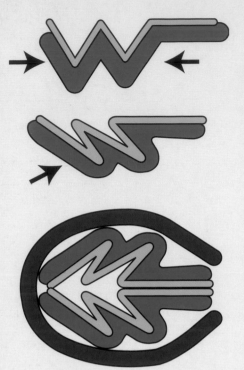

1 Laying fiber for the leaves

Lay out a layer of Fiber B on the sushi mat making a 7" (18cm) square. Add 3 more layers of Fiber B, each perpendicular to the last. Add 2 layers of Fiber A to the fiber stack, again changing direction with each new layer of fiber. Pull the stack apart into 2 equal 3½" × 7" (9cm × 18cm) pieces. Fold each stack into 2 ridges to create the veins of the leaves.

Bend the folds so that the veins point toward the tip of the forming leaf shape.

Wrap the leaf shape with a layer of Fiber C.

2 Felting the leaves

Wet the fiber roll thoroughly with warm, soapy water. Because the desired finished shape for this piece is not a cylinder, you won't be able to roll the fibers to felt them. Instead, fold the sushi mat over the fibers and rock it back and forth while applying pressure to create friction. Check every few minutes to see if the piece has felted; add warm, soapy water if the piece gets cold. Continue rocking until the fibers are completely felted together. Rinse the felt in cool water and squeeze out any excess water in a dry towel. Shape the felt if needed and allow it to dry completely.

3 Laying fiber for the flower

Lay out a layer of Fiber D on the sushi mat making a 7" (18cm) square. Add 3 more layers of Fiber D, each perpendicular to the last. Add 2 layers of Fiber E to the fiber stack, again changing direction with each new layer of fiber. Roll the fibers tightly into a jelly roll.

4 Felting the flower

Felt the flower fiber roll (see *Flat Felting, Step by Step*, pages 42–47).When the piece is felted, shape it and let it dry completely.

5 Finishing

When the leaf and flower felt rolls are completely dry, cut each roll into 1" (3cm) pieces with a very sharp knife. If the fibers toward the center of each roll are not felted together, use a felting needle to felt them completely. To finish felting, you can also rewet the pieces and roll them in the sushi mat to felt and flatten them.

Millefiori Beads

The technique used to create this project is commonly used in polymer clay projects, but originates from fine glass beads made in Italy. "Millefiori" translates into English as "a thousand flowers," a name inspired by the appearance of the Italian glass beads, which in turn inspired this project. These beautiful felt beads are wonderful surprises, because it's always exciting to cut them apart and see the unique centers that have formed.

The round beads shown at left were made using Harrisville Designs Fleece in the following colors: 067 Marigold (A), 021 Violet (B), 031 Cobalt (C), 002 Red (D), 023 Magenta (E), 024 Periwinkle (F), 033 Midnight (G) and 044 White (H).
The oval beads shown at left were made using Harrisville Designs Fleece in the following colors: 067 Marigold (A), 033 Midnight (G), 011 Emerald (I) and 009 Evergreen (J).

Round Beads

SKILL LEVEL

Beginner

FINISHED SIZE

Diameter: Approx.
  1¼" (3cm)

MATERIALS

1⅔ oz. (46g) feltable
  wool fiber in 8
  colors: 6g of Fiber
  A; 12g of Fiber B; 4g
  each of Fibers C, D,
  E and F; 10g of Fiber
  G; 2g of Fiber H

Size 36 felting needle

Felting mat

Sushi mat

Warm, soapy water

Rubberbands

Cool water for rinsing

Dry towel

Sharp knife

Cutting board

1 Begin laying the fibers

Lay out a 2" × 6" (5cm × 15cm) layer of Fiber B on the felting mat. Roll a 1" × 6" (3cm × 15cm) length of Fiber A in your hands until it compacts into a thin rope. Lay the rope of Fiber A on the felting mat and cover it with Fiber B. Use the felting needle to secure Fiber B completely around Fiber A. Repeat 2 times.

Hold the 3 fiber logs together and wrap them tightly in a 2" × 6" (5cm × 15cm) layer of Fiber C. Needle the overlaps so that the piece is secure and tightly wrapped.

2 Continue laying fibers

Roll 2" × 6" (5cm × 15cm) lengths of Fibers D, E and F in your hands until each compacts into a thin rope. Hold these ropes along with the fiber log you already made, and wrap them all together tightly in a 2" × 6" (5cm × 15cm) layer of Fiber G. Needle the overlaps so that the piece is secure and tightly wrapped.

Wrap this log with a 1" × 6" (3cm × 15cm) length of Fiber H that goes only half way around the log, then wrap the whole log, including Fiber H, in a 3" × 6" (8cm × 15cm) layer of Fiber G. For each layer, needle the piece tightly with the felting needle so that you have a dense form that holds its shape.

3 Felting

Felt the fiber roll (see *Flat Felting, Step by Step*, pages 42–47). When the piece is felted, shape it and let it dry completely.

4 Finishing

When the felt roll is completely dry, cut it into 1" (3cm) pieces with a very sharp knife. For a different look, try cutting pieces at an angle. If the fibers toward the center of the roll are not felted together, use a felting needle to felt them completely. To finish felting, you can also rewet the pieces and roll them in the sushi mat to felt and flatten them.

Oval Beads

SKILL LEVEL

Beginner

FINISHED SIZE

Approx. ¾" × 2"

(2cm × 5cm)

MATERIALS

¾ oz. (22g) feltable
   wool fiber in 4
   colors, 4g each of
   Fibers A, G and I;
   10g of Fiber J

Hand carders
   (optional)

Size 36 felting needle

Felting mat

Sushi mat

Warm, soapy water

Rubberbands

Cool water for rinsing

Dry towel

Sharp knife

Cutting board

1 **Laying the fibers**
If desired, make a fiber blend by hand carding 2g of Fiber A with a pinch of Fiber I. Shape this blend (or your fiber of choice) into a 1" × 6" (3cm × 15cm) length of fiber and roll it in your hands until it compacts into a thin rope. Make a second rope of the same size with Fiber A. Roll a 2" × 6" (5cm × 15cm) length of Fiber I in your hands until it compacts into a rope. Wrap these 3 ropes tightly together in a 2" × 6" (5cm × 15cm) layer of Fiber G. Needle the overlaps so that the piece is secure and tightly wrapped.

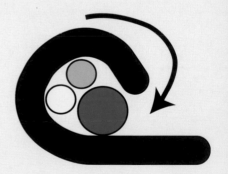

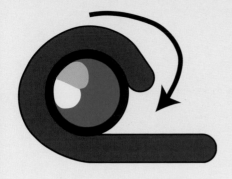

2 Finish roll
Wrap the log made in Step 1 with a 3" × 6" (8cm × 15cm) layer of Fiber J and needle the layers tightly together.

3 Felting
Felt the fiber roll (see *Flat Felting, Step by Step*, pages 42–47). When the piece is felted, press down along one side of the roll so that the felt roll is formed into a teardrop shape. Allow the roll to dry completely.

4 Finishing
When the felt roll is completely dry, cut it into 1" (3cm) pieces with a very sharp knife. Cut the pieces at an angle. If the fibers toward the center of the roll are not felted together, use a felting needle to felt them completely. To finish felting, you can also rewet the pieces and roll them in the sushi mat to felt and flatten them.

Using the Millefiori Beads

Once you have completed a set of Millefiori Beads, they can be used in numerous ways. String them in jewelry, just as you would for any other bead, or use them as embellishments. I used one bead as the focal point for this necklace and completed the look with beads that matched the fibers used in the Millefiori Beads.

Knotted Netting Scarf

One way to add stability to a felted item is to include a mesh in the fibers as you lay them out. The hand-knotted mesh used in this project adds structure to the light cobweb felt and creates a pretty pattern in the scarf. Try adding beads to the knotting or paint the wet fibers with dye to further embellish this project.

The project shown at left was made using Lorna's Laces Shepherd Wooltop in the Irving Park colorway and Lorna's Laces Bullfrogs and Butterflies (85% wool, 15% mohair, 4 oz./113g, 190 yd./174m) in the Tahoe colorway.

SKILL LEVEL
Intermediate

FINISHED SIZE
Approx. 7" × 54"
  (18cm × 137cm)
  without fringe

MATERIALS
4 oz. (113g) feltable
  wool fiber
1 (4 oz./113g, 190
  yd./174m) skein
  feltable wool yarn
Straight pins
Bubble wrap
Netting (optional)
Warm, soapy water
Dowel rod
Rubberbands
Cool water for rinsing
Dry towel

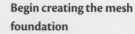

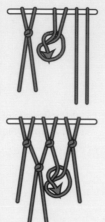

1 **Begin creating the mesh foundation**

Cut 6 60" (152cm) lengths of yarn. Tie 1 end of each strand to a dowel rod. Tie the 1st and 2nd strands together in an overhand knot 3" (8cm) below the dowel rod. Repeat with the 3rd and 4th strands, as well as the 5th and 6th.

Work the next row of knots by skipping the 1st strand and tying the 2nd and 3rd strands together 3" (8cm) below the first set of knots. Repeat with the 4th and 5th strands of yarn.

2 **Continue mesh foundation**

Repeat the 1st 2 rows of knotting to the end of the yarn strands. Cut the yarn approximately 1" (3cm) before the 1st row of knots and after the last row of knots.

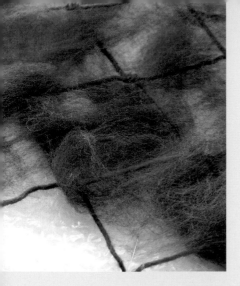

3 Lay out the fibers

Spread a thin layer of wool fibers over a 12" × 55" (30cm × 140cm) area on top of bubble wrap. Carefully lay the yarn mesh over the fibers, arranging it so it covers the fibers completely. Pin the edges of the yarn mesh to the bubble wrap. Spread another thin layer of fibers over the mesh in the opposite direction from the 1st.

4 Felt the scarf

Felt the scarf (see *Flat Felting, Step by Step*, pages 42–47). While felting the scarf, occasionally unroll the bundle and check to see that the fibers are not too sparse. Add more fiber where needed. Gently push the ends of the fibers in along the sides of the scarf to form smooth edges on the scarf. Use a steam iron to heat the fibers while felting. Continue to check the progress, steam and reroll the scarf until the fibers are felted to each other through the mesh. Remove the pins from the bubble wrap and felt the scarf further in the sink by kneading it and adding warm, soapy water as needed. Rinse gently in cool water and press out extra moisture with a clean, dry towel. Allow the felt to dry completely. If desired, add fringe to the ends of the scarf. Cut 30 17" (43cm) strands of yarn. Knot 5 strands together at each knot in the yarn mesh at each end of the scarf.

Nuno Scarf

This project uses a wool-blend scarf blank as a foundation for light layers of wool fiber that gently gather the fabric during felting. Working with a ready-made scarf allows you to enjoy the felting process without any finishing tasks after the felting is complete. The colorwash appearance of this scarf is created by overlapping the different colors at each color change. Try this scarf in your favorite colors!

The project shown at left was made using Harrisville Designs Fleece in the following colors: 012 Sea Green (A), 017 Bermuda Blue (B) and 024 Periwinkle (C).

SKILL LEVEL
Beginner

FINISHED SIZE
Approx. 7" × 48"
(18cm × 122cm)

MATERIALS
6 oz. (170g) feltable
    wool fiber in 3 colors
    (A, B and C), 2 oz.
    (57g) each
12" × 60 "
    (30cm × 152cm)
    wool-blend scarf
Bubble wrap
Netting (optional)
Warm, soapy water
Dowel rod
Rubberbands
Cool water for rinsing
Dry towel

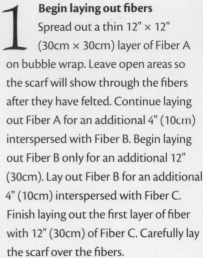

1 Begin laying out fibers

Spread out a thin 12" × 12" (30cm × 30cm) layer of Fiber A on bubble wrap. Leave open areas so the scarf will show through the fibers after they have felted. Continue laying out Fiber A for an additional 4" (10cm) interspersed with Fiber B. Begin laying out Fiber B only for an additional 12" (30cm). Lay out Fiber B for an additional 4" (10cm) interspersed with Fiber C. Finish laying out the first layer of fiber with 12" (30cm) of Fiber C. Carefully lay the scarf over the fibers.

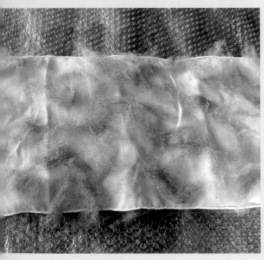

2 Finish laying out fibers

Spread a thin layer of fibers on top of the scarf. Follow the same color order used in Step 1.

3 Felt the scarf

Felt the scarf (see *Flat Felting, Step by Step*, pages 42–47). While felting the scarf, open the bundle and wrap any fibers extending beyond the scarf around the edges of the scarf, so the sides and ends of the scarf are even. Use a steam iron to heat the fibers while felting. Continue to check the progress, steam and reroll the scarf until the fibers are felted to each other through the scarf. Felt the scarf further in the sink by kneading it and adding warm, soapy water as needed. Rinse gently in cool water and press out extra moisture with a clean, dry towel. Allow the felt to dry completely.

Ruched Nuno Tunic

This lightweight tunic is a great project for those who like to sew and it shows off the wonderful qualities of Nuno felting. By using the feltable fibers sparingly, areas of open fabric will be left that will contrast beautifully with the ruched felted areas. The flowing ruffle at the bottom edge of the piece is created by the gathering effect of the felting.

The project shown at left was made using Ashland Bay Merino Tencel in the Peacock colorway and Multicolor Firestar Nylon in the Green colorway.

SKILL LEVEL

Intermediate

FINISHED SIZE

Approx. 36" (1m)
  at bust

MATERIALS

2 oz. (57g) feltable
  wool-blend fiber

1 oz. (28g) nylon fiber

2 yd. (2m) sheer fabric

Sewing machine and
  thread

Fitted T-shirt

Bamboo mat

Netting (optional)

Thick, flexible plastic
  sheet

Warm, soapy water

Dowel rod

Rubberbands

Cool water for rinsing

Dry towel

2 tennis balls
  (optional)

Clothes dryer
  (optional)

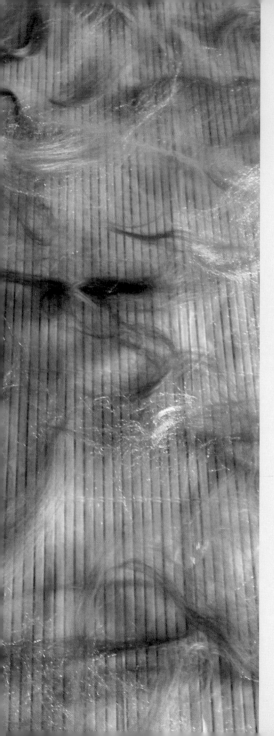

1 Begin laying out the first layer of fibers

Lay out a sparse layer of the wool-blend and nylon fibers over the bamboo mat, covering an area approximately 4" (10cm) narrower than the width of the fabric you're using and 24" (61cm) shorter than the fabric.

2 Finish laying out the fibers

Carefully lay the fabric over the fibers, aligining the fabric so that it has a 12" (30cm) margin at the top and bottom of the fiber and a 2" (5cm) margin on each side. Lay out another layer of wool-blend and nylon fibers on top of the fabric, mirroring the bottom layer of fiber.

3 Felt the fabric

Felt the fibers to the fabric (see *Flat Felting, Step by Step*, pages 42–47). While felting, occasionally open up the bundle and check to see if the fibers have shifted and to see if the fibers are felted.

Felt the fabric further in the sink by kneading it and adding warm soapy water as needed. Rinse in cool water and squeeze out excess water in a clean dry towel. To gather the fabric more, place the fabric in a clothes dryer with 2 tennis balls for 10–20 minutes on a warm/hot setting.

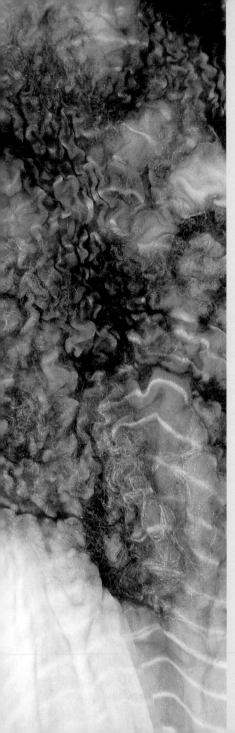

4 Sew the tunic

Fold the fabric in half so that the selvages are along the sides and the 12" (30cm) areas of unfelted fabric meet. Trim the unfelted fabric to approximately 7" (18cm). Turn the bottom edge of each piece of unfelted fabric under twice and hem.

Following the illustration below, and a fitted T-shirt as a guide, sew the sleeve and arm seams. Cut a V shaped opening for the neckline. Use the excess unfelted fabric to make a 1" (3cm) wide facing; sew the facing over the neckline.

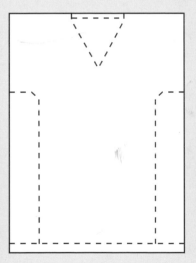

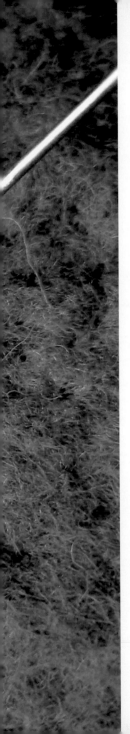

Needle Felting

Needle felting is different from the other felting processes in this book because it is a dry felting method. Rather than using steam or warm, soapy water, in needle felting the fibers are physically pushed together, forcing them to lock and mat. This technique can be used to produce two-dimensional work, such as the Landscape Painting *on page 138, or three-dimensional work like the* Olde World Santa *on page 146. Although this process works best with wool, it can also be used to felt wool fiber to another type of surface. For example, the* Lamb Tote Bag *on page 126 features wool fibers felted to cotton canvas. Acrylic craft felt is made commercially by needle felting, and in fact, the felting needles crafters use come from the felt-making industry, which uses large beds of felting needles to form fibers into felt for all sorts of industrial uses in addition to craft felt.*

The Basics of Needle Felting

Needle felting is the simple process of needling, or poking fibers with a felting needle, so that they become embedded in other fibers or to a surface. For both surface design and sculpture, there are several techniques that can be used, and each produces a different effect. Try playing around with some fiber and a felting needle to find which techniques work best for you.

Needling

Felting needles are three- or four-sided needles, which are very sharp and brittle and have barbs along each edge. These barbs catch fibers as you move the needle up and down through the fiber mass, tangling and matting the fibers together.

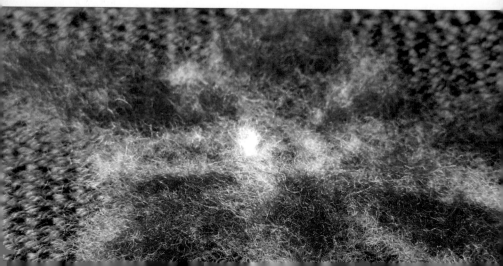

I recommend using a padded surface under a project while you work so you can push the felting needle through the background fiber or fabric to securely anchor the fibers in place. A felting mat, foam padding, styrofoam or any padded surface that doesn't get felted easily all make great work surfaces. A felting mat gives less resistance to the needling than foam padding, making the felting easier, but the back of the project will be fuzzier than a project worked on top of foam padding. A good compromise is a felting mat covered with an old towel; this creates some resistance, but not as much as foam padding. Remember to frequently lift the project up from the work surface so that the fibers don't get felted to the padding or mat.

If you are not working on a felting mat, it's a good idea to wear a leather glove on the hand that will be holding the fibers to prevent painful needle pokes. Be very careful when handling felting needles; their barbs make them more dangerous than a normal needle.

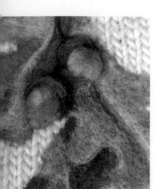

Surface Design

Creating needle-felted surface designs is like painting with
fibers. You can create a design with lines, use shading to make
subtle color transitions and add dimensional effects through
layering or selective needling.

When working on the surface of a project to add color or
decorative elements, use needle plunges that are about ½"–1"
(1cm–3cm) deep. Skimming the surface of the project with
more shallow plunges of the needle is a good way to blend
fiber colors smoothly or to make a smooth transition from an
added element to the base of the project. Picking at the fibers
with a felting needle can be used to move fibers or to separate
colors so they blend better, but be gentle with the needle so
you don't break it. The surface of a project can be hardened by
light needling with ¼"–½" (6mm–13mm) deep plunges over
the entire surface of the fiber.

To create deep indentations or dimension in a piece,
plunge the needle more deeply to get the fibers to lock
together into the desired form. Angling a single felting needle
approximately 45 degrees from the surface of the piece can
also help to create dimensional objects, or can be used to
blend sections of fiber together or to define edges. I don't
recommend working at an angle when using a felting needle
holder with more than one felting needle because this tends
to bend the needles, which can then break.

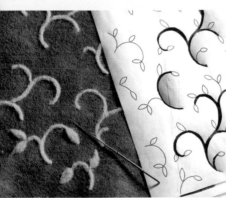

Transferring Patterns

There are several ways to transfer a pattern to your work. For many projects in this book, the first step will be to enlarge the design on a photocopier.

If the project calls for needle felting onto a fabric background, once the pattern has been enlarged to the appropriate size, layer a piece of carbon paper on the fabric backing and place the pattern over the carbon paper. Trace over the pattern lines so they transfer to the background fabric.

If you are working on a surface that won't show carbon paper lines, a template can be a very helpful tool. When creating a template for needle felting, you are using the part of the pattern that would normally be thrown away. You cut out the design and use the surrounding paper for your template, so that you are needling inside an opening rather than around a pattern shape. Make a copy of the pattern on text-weight paper or freezer paper, then cut along the pattern lines. Pin a text-weight paper template to the piece, or iron a freezer paper template onto the surface of your project. Needle fiber to the surface following the inside edges of the pattern. Once the basic pattern has been applied, remove the template and finish defining the design.

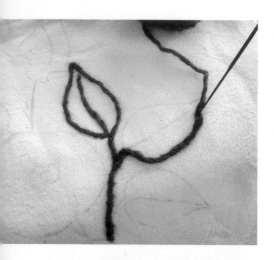

Creating a Line Design

Outlining a pattern is a great way to make a repeating pattern that needs to be uniform. You can also outline a pattern with a contrasting color to accentuate a design.

Outlining a simple design with yarn is a great introduction to needle felting. I like to use single-ply wool yarn, because it doesn't show the needle holes. If you use a plied yarn, it shows the needle holes and looks as if you damaged the yarn to get it in place. I needle mostly along the side edges of the yarn so that there are not any noticeable holes poked into the middle of the yarn. This makes a nice clean line, and raises the yarn up slightly, creating nice textural interest. Don't cut the ends of the yarn until you are sure how long you want them. Then cut them a little longer than you intend them to be and needle them down heavily so they stay in place.

There are two methods for making a crisp outline of your pattern. One is to place a small amount of fiber inside the design area, then needle in place, taking special care to make a crisp, clean outline following the edges of the template.

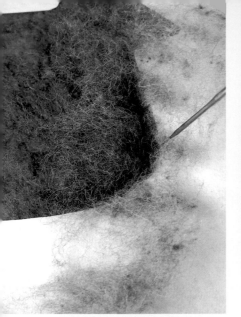

The other method is to lay an airy, loose tuft of fiber over the pattern so that it overlaps the edge of the pattern. If your fibers are worsted, you will need to jumble them up by rubbing them between your fingers so that they are not laying in one direction, but tangled slightly. You only need a wispy amount of fiber at this point, so you should be able to easily see through the fiber and it should be a contrasting color to the background fabric. Needle straight up and down along the pattern line, working either back and forth or in a progressive line, as if you are creating a line with dots. The fibers will begin to form a line. Fold any loose fiber that is hanging over the paper back into the center of the pattern and continue needling further into the center of the pattern until you have a clear outline of the design. Remove the pattern and needle in the remaining fibers in the center of the design, adding more fiber as needed for complete coverage.

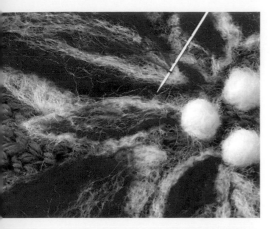

Shading

After you have a basic pattern needled in place, you can enhance the design through shading. Shading adds depth and dimension to a design. Only a small amount of fiber is needed for subtle shading, so that you can see the color below, giving more depth to the color changes.

Fluff up a very small amount of fiber and place it where you want your color change. Needle from the center out to the edges, pulling and adjusting the fibers as needed to create a smooth color transition. If you make a mistake, you can either pull the fibers off or cover the mistake with additional fibers. That's the beauty of needle felting! Building up colors adds to the design. If you want a direction to your fibers, you can use worsted fibers as they are, without fluffing them between your fingers. They will keep their directional lines in the finished design.

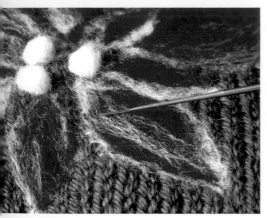

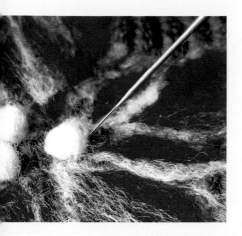

Adding Dimension

To give a design element a padded or raised effect, use two or three times as much fiber as needed for a flat element. Begin by lightly needling in the center of the element just enough to hold the fiber in place. Next, needle only around the edges of the raised element, needling at a 45-degree angle from the surface of the work so that the added fiber stays raised up from the surface with only the edge tightly adhered to the background. From slightly padded designs to highly dimensional elements, the technique remains the same with only the amount of fiber changing. You can also create dimensional elements separately, then add them to the surface by needling them onto the main project.

Sculptures

One of the reasons I love needle felting is that it can be used to create beautiful sculptures with fiber. The creative possibilities are endless, but every three-dimensional needle-felted piece begins with a base form. For more complicated forms, an armature made from wire or pipe cleaners is helpful for forming the piece. For simple shapes, a bundle of fiber is a great start. Once the basic form is created, you then build on it to create your finished piece.

Armatures

Using wire or pipe cleaners, create the basic shape of your finished piece. Spend time with the design of the wire form so that it will do everything you need it to do for the finished sculpture. Taking care at this stage will save you time and frustration later in the process. The armature needs to help hold the shape of the piece as well as balance it so it is sturdy and stable. Make sure the wires are long enough for the limbs of a human or animal sculpture and fold over any cut ends so that they won't poke through the finished piece. Wrap wool around the armature and needle it until it stays in place. For the interior of the sculpture, you can save money by using natural colored fiber, which is less expensive than dyed fibers. You don't have to felt every part of the interior fibers into dense felt, but make sure to felt the fibers enough to get them to stay in place. Once the armature is complete, you are ready to add details to the project.

Bundles of Fiber

For a soft sculpture with a simple form, a bundle of fibers can serve as the base. To make such a base, ball up enough fiber to approximately reach the desired size of your piece, lightly needling it together so that it holds its shape. While needling, I also cup the fiber in my hands and gently breathe on it to warm the fibers and help them mat together slightly. As you work the fibers, shape them into the basic shape you desire for your finished piece. When the shape is formed you are ready to add to it to make your finished piece.

Altering the Base Shape

To alter the basic shape of your base, you can begin needling heavily in one location to create an indentation, or you can pinch and hold the base to the desired shape, and needle it until it stays that way.

Adding Elements

Once the base shape of your form is complete, you can add further dimensional elements to the form, such as adding a nose to a face, by first forming them, then needling them in place. Winding wool around a stick, then sliding it off the stick, is a good way to add shaping. You can also fold the fiber to create three-dimensional shapes that you needle in place along the edges. Whenever you plan to form a separate element to add to a piece, always leave a small tuft of fiber unfelted so you have a surface to needle to your base.

Shading

Once all of the dimensional aspects of a sculpture are complete, the surface design can begin (see *Surface Design*, pages 106–111). You can add shading at any time while working on your base shape. Subtle and dramatic color changes can also be added when you've just about completed your piece. Color changes can be added into the elements you join to the base by mixing the fiber colors before making them into added elements for the sculpture. Finally, you can even paint the finished piece with dye to create highly detailed accents.

MATERIALS

½ oz. (14g) white feltable wool fiber

½ oz. (14g) flesh-tone feltable wool fiber

1 oz. (28g) feltable wool fiber or longwool locks for hair

Small amounts of feltable wool fiber in assorted colors for eyes and other facial details

Toothpick

Size 38 or 40 felting needle

Felting mat

Step-by-Step Faces

Needle-felted sculptures of people are a very popular item, but many beginning needle felters find them challenging. Faces are a special type of sculpture that have a structure all their own. Many felt artists have their own process for creating faces. Here is the method I use to make a 4" (10cm) face.

1 Base bundle

Make a slightly flattened, rounded bundle of fiber about 3" (8cm) across using white fiber. The base color will show through at the eyes, so make sure to use white wool.

Use the desired skin color for the remaining steps.

2 Lower eyelids

Make 4 1" (3cm) wide rolls of flesh-tone fiber on a toothpick. Arch two of them and needle them in place at the center of the bundle as shown. These are the lower eyelids.

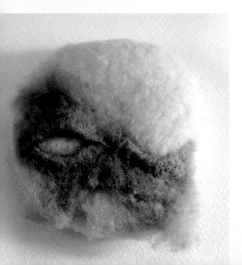

3 Upper eyelids

Arch the remaining 2 rolls of fiber and slightly overlap the edges of the 1st 2 rolls of fiber as shown, and needle them in place.

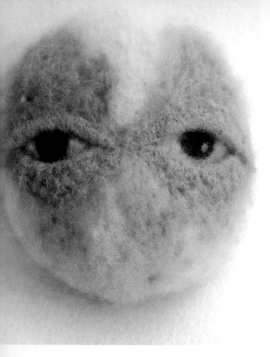

4 Adding eyes

Using a very small amount of fiber, needle a flat circle in the center of the eye for the iris. The circle should be partly hidden at the top of the eye. For the pupil, add an even smaller black circle to the upper center of the iris so that the black dot is just touching the top eyelid. Then, add a very small dot of white to the lower right or left section of the pupil—be sure to place it in the same place on both eyes. This represents a reflection of light off the eye.

5 First half of mouth

Make 2 1½" (4cm) wide rolls of flesh-tone fiber. Arch 1 roll and needle it in place; carefully shape the lip as you needle to form the facial expression you desire. For a smile, attach the top lip first. For a frown, attach the bottom lip first. Form the cupped shape that is below the nose by needling the fiber there.

6 Second half of mouth

Arch the 2nd roll and needle it in place, slightly overlapping the edges of the 1st. Work carefully to form the desired facial expression.

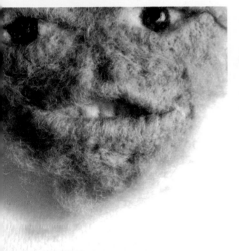

7 Adding teeth

For the teeth, you can either work on the base bundle, or add more fiber between the lips. Carefully needle the fiber between the lips to form the indentations around the teeth. If you want to show empty spaces between the teeth, needle in a small amount of black or brown.

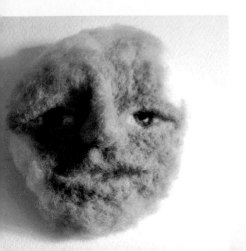

8 Nose

Fold a 2" (5cm) length of fiber to form a triangle point at 1 end, with the fiber tips at the other end of the triangle. Place this in the center of the face and needle in place. Use additional needling to form the nose into the desired shape.

9 Adding the forehead

Make a 3" (8cm) roll of flesh-tone fiber on a skewer and place it above the eyes. Needle at an angle towards the eye so that the curve is more subtle than it was for the lips or eyelids.

10 Adding details

Finish covering the front and sides of the face with flesh-tone fiber and begin adding the finishing touches to the face. Add more flesh-tone fiber for a larger chin or cheeks. Add wrinkles, if desired, by needling lines across the forehead and around the eyes and mouth. You can also add color to the lips, blush to the cheeks and eye makeup, too!

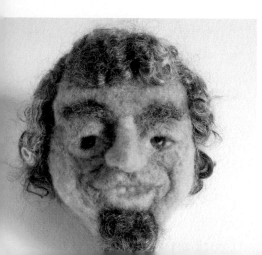

11 Adding hair

Fill out the back of the head, which may be flattened from all the needling on the front. Add eyebrows and hair to the face. Locks of wool are a great choice, but you can also wrap roving around the head to create a bun or other close hair design.

Tips for Success

— If you are holding a project in your hand while working, wear a snug-fitting leather glove on the hand holding the fiber so you are less likely to poke your hand with the felting needle.

— To help the wool compress and felt together, cup it in your hands and gently breathe on it to warm and dampen the fibers slightly, which will help them mat together better.

— Never needle felt wet fibers. The needles will break more easily, and since the needles are steel, they can rust.

— Unfortunately, when starting out in needle felting it is almost inevitable that you will stab yourself with those sharp needles at least once, so have first aid supplies on hand and keep your tetanus shot up to date.

Floral Tote Bag

With just a few simple tools and a single-ply yarn, you can try your hand at needle felting while dressing up a simple canvas bag. This easy project can be adapted to almost any line design to create a beautiful bag. Although you can complete this pattern by choosing several single-color skeins of yarn in the colors you need, a variegated yarn containing most or all of the colors in the design can also be a great choice. By using a variegated yarn, I completed this design with just one ball of yarn.

The project shown at left was made using Noro Kureyon (100% wool, 1¾ oz./50g, 110 yd./100m) color #154.

SKILL LEVEL
Beginner

FINISHED SIZE
Needle felting covers a 7" × 8" (18cm × 20cm) area

MATERIALS
1 (1¾ oz./50g, 110 yd./100m) skein variegated single-ply feltable worsted weight yarn containing your desired colors OR 1 skein single-ply worsted weight yarn in each of your desired colors

12" × 12" (30cm × 30cm) canvas tote bag

Size 36 felting needle

Felting mat

Scissors

Pattern transfer supplies

1 Transfer design

Enlarge the pattern (see page 125) to the recommended size, or to a custom size to fit your tote bag. Transfer the floral pattern to the canvas bag (see *Transferring Patterns*, page 107).

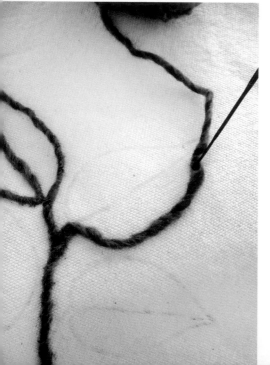

2 Felt design

Place the felting mat inside the canvas bag under the area to be embellished. Begin attaching the yarn to the canvas bag following the pattern, cutting the yarn at the end of each line after it is attached to the canvas. Move the felting mat often to keep it under the section you are working on and to keep the fibers from sticking into the mat. Continue felting strands until the design is outlined. Then, fill in the interior of the design. Be careful to make sure the ends of each strand are securely embedded in the canvas.

Enlarge to 225% to bring to full size.

Lamb Tote Bag

This little lamb fit perfectly between the straps of a canvas bag I purchased, but you can enlarge or shrink the design to make it fit anything you choose. For a creative twist, try decorating the lamb with loose wool fibers instead of swirls of yarn.

The project shown at left was made using Brown Sheep Lamb's Pride Worsted (85% wool/15% mohair, 4 oz./113g, 190 yd./174m), 1 skein in color MV260 Cafe Au Lait and 1 skein in color M05 Onyx.

SKILL LEVEL

Beginner

FINISHED SIZE

Needle felting covers a 4" × 6" (10cm × 15cm) area

MATERIALS

1 (4 oz./113g, 190 yd./174m) skein single-ply feltable worsted weight yarn (A)

1 (4 oz./113g, 190 yd./174m) skein variegated single-ply feltable worsted weight yarn (B)

12" × 12" (30cm × 30cm) canvas tote bag

Size 36 felting needle

Felting mat

Scissors

Pattern transfer supplies

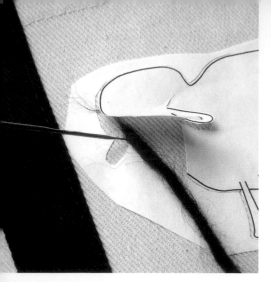

1 Transfer design

Enlarge the pattern (see page 129) to the recommended size, or to a custom size to fit your tote bag. Transfer the pattern to the canvas bag (see *Transferring Patterns*, page 107).

2 Felt design

Place the felting mat inside the canvas bag under the area to be embellished. Using the pattern (see page 129), begin attaching Yarn A to the canvas bag starting with the head and ears. Cut the yarn at the end of each line after it is attached to the canvas. Move the felting mat often to keep it under the section you are working on and to keep the fibers from sticking into the mat. Continue by felting the legs and the tail with Yarn A. Then, fill in the interior of the design with spirals of Yarn B. Be careful to make sure the ends of each strand are securely embedded in the canvas.

Pattern outline
Enlarge to 225% to bring to full size.

Filled pattern
Enlarge to 225% to bring to full size.

Pedestal Pin Cushion

Although this project can be made into any type of pin cushion, I like having it in a container with a lid to keep dust off of the wool. Because this pattern has a lot of points and curves, it requires a sharp outline, but a little extra care will help ensure your success. This two-color design can also be repeated and worked on a variety of projects to add a decorative flair.

SKILL LEVEL

Intermediate

FINISHED SIZE

Needle felting covers a 4" × 4" (10cm × 10cm) area

MATERIALS

2½ oz. (71g) feltable wool fiber in 2 colors, 2 oz. (57g) of Fiber A and ½ oz. (14g) of Fiber B

Size 36 felting needles

Felting needle holder

Felting mat

Lidded pedestal container

Pattern transfer supplies

Thick white glue

1 Felt base fibers

Arrange Fiber A into a round batt with a 6" (15cm) diameter approximately 3" (8cm) thick. Using a felting needle holder with several needles attached and felting mat, needle felt the batt until the center compacts to about 1" (3cm) thick. Do not felt the edges of the batt.

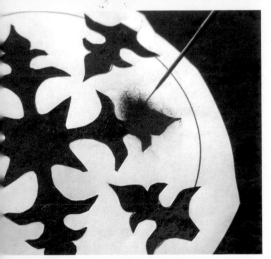

2 Transfer design

Transfer the pattern on page 133 to the batt you've just created (see *Transferring Patterns*, page 107). Begin filling in the pattern by needle felting with Fiber B and a single felting needle (see *Creating a Line Design*, pages 108–109).

3 Finish design

Once the pattern is filled, remove the pattern paper and refine the edges of the design. Turn the edges of the fiber batt under and glue the fiber into the pin cushion base with thick white glue. Allow the glue to dry completely before using the pin cushion.

Pattern shown at actual size.

Fish Bowl Felting Needle Holder

When I first saw this candle holder, it struck me that it looked just like a miniature fish bowl. The idea to needle felt a pattern you could see through the glass popped into my head and this project was born. You could also needle felt this design flat on a thin fiber batt and slide it into a container, then place a smaller container in the middle to create a pencil holder or vase.

The project shown at left was made using Harrisville Designs Fleece in the following colors: 030 Azure, 043 Sand, 002 Red, 011 Emerald, 008 Hemlock and 067 Marigold.

SKILL LEVEL

Intermediate

FINISHED SIZE

3" × 3" × 3" (8cm × 8cm × 8cm)

MATERIALS

2 oz. (57g) feltable wool fiber for water

Feltable wool fiber in 5 colors for embellishments, less than 1 oz. (28g) each

3" × 3" × 3" (8cm × 8cm × 8cm) round glass container

Size 36 felting needle

Felting mat

Pattern transfer supplies

Hand carders (optional)

1 Blend fiber (optional)

You can use a solid color to represent the water in this project, but I think a blend looks more realistic. If you like, blend blue and green fibers with hand carders to reach the shade you desire for the "water" in your fish bowl.

2 Needle felt fibers

Roll the fiber you've chosen for the water into a tight ball a little larger than the glass container. Needle over the entire surface of the ball until it is even and has a firm surface. Needle a 2½" (6cm) circle of fiber to the bottom of the fiber ball to represent sand.

Enlarge the pattern (see page 137) to the recommended size. Transfer the pattern to the ball of fiber, roughly lining up the sand on the pattern and fiber ball so that the plants are growing out of the sand and the crab is standing on the sand (see *Transferring Patterns*, page 107). Needle felt the fibers following the pattern, carefully defining the edges of each shape. Squeeze the finished piece into the glass container. If the fiber ball became too small during felting to entirely fill the container, make a hole in the top center of the ball and stuff more fiber inside until the ball fits snuggly in the container.

Enlarge to 150% to bring to full size.

Enlarge to 150% to bring to full size.

Landscape Painting

Creating a landscape painting is a great way to try out different effects when you're experimenting with a new medium. Use the pattern provided or choose a composition that explores many texture and color changes so you can try a wide range of techniques. If you don't have any inspiring scenery locally, try using a photo of a landscape for this project.

SKILL LEVEL

Beginner

FINISHED SIZE

9 "× 16"

(23cm × 41cm)

MATERIALS

4 oz. (113g)

feltable wool fiber
in a variety of colors
appropriate for a
sunset

Size 36 felting needles

Felting needle holder

Felting mat

Pattern transfer
supplies

The project shown at left was made using Lorna's Laces Shepherd Wooltop in the Irving Park colorway.

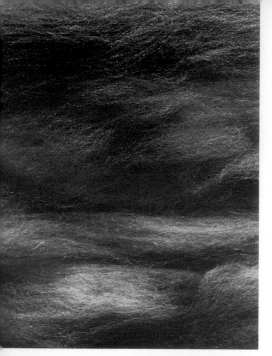

1 Create background

Lay out a layer of the lightest colored fiber, forming a batt approximately 10" ×17" (25cm × 43cm) with all the fibers lying in the same direction. Lay a 2nd layer of light fibers perpendicular to the 1st. Lay out a 3rd layer with the fibers parallel to the 1st layer. Add purple fiber at the top, and add reds and small amounts of purple to the middle section, imitating the appearance of the sky at sunset.

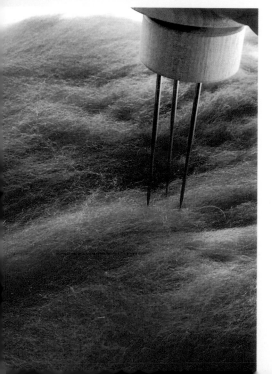

2 Create landscape

Enlarge the pattern (see page 141) to the recommended size. Transfer the pattern to the background batt (see *Transferring Patterns*, page 107). Lay out additional fibers following the pattern to form a sunset image. Press the fibers down with your hands so they compact a little. Lift a corner of the batt up and slide the felting mat under the fibers. Begin needle felting, working over the entire batt. Move the felting mat often to keep it under the section you are working on and to keep the fibers from sticking into the mat. Needle felt the piece until the fibers are completely matted together.

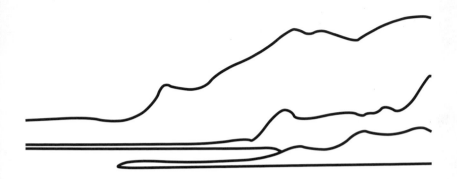

Enlarge to 200% to bring to full size.

Creating an Original Landscape

Try creating a felted landscape depicting your favorite place. Create a line drawing from a photo of that place for your pattern and add as many (or as few) details as you like. Try to create different textures and effects by varying the amount of needling you use as well as the depth of your needle jabs.

Itty Bitty Kitty

Needle-felted miniatures are fun to make for children and adults alike. This diminutive cat is as cute as can be, and you can personalize yours by choosing colors to match your favorite feline.

The projects shown at left were made using Harrisville Designs Fleece in the following colors: 040 Topaz, 041 Sandalwood and 038 Teak.

SKILL LEVEL
Intermediate

FINISHED SIZE
6½" × 3" × 1½"
  (17cm × 8cm × 4cm)

MATERIALS
¼ oz. (7g) feltable
  wool fiber
Small amounts of
  feltable wool fiber
  in several colors for
  facial features
Size 38, 40 or 42
  felting needle
Felting mat

1 Begin sculpture

Set a 1" (3cm) pinch of fiber aside for the neck, then divide the remaining fiber into 4 equal sections. Needle felt 1 section of fiber into a log approximately 2½" × 1¼" (6cm × 3cm).

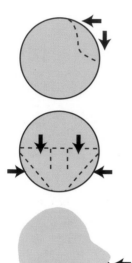

2 Form head

Divide the 2nd section of fiber in half. Needle felt the 1st half into a 1¼" (3cm) diameter ball to form the kitty's head. Needle felt the ball forming a deep indent around half of the ball. This indent will become the area where the eyes and nose will be added.

Needle felt along the sides of the nose to create a raised ridge in the center of the nose area. Needle felt inward at the sides of the nose to form the face into a cat-like shape.

Needle felt the face to form shallow indentations along the muzzle to form a mouth.

Pull 2 small tufts off of the unfelted portion of the 2nd fiber section for the ears. Fold the tufts into thirds so that a triangle shape is created with a point at one end and loose fiber at the other end. Needle felt the ears until they are firm at the point section. Place them on the back of the head and needle them in place.

Roll the remaining unfelted fiber from the 2nd section between your hands to make the tail. The tail needs to be pointed at one end and loose fiber at the other so you can needle felt it in place later.

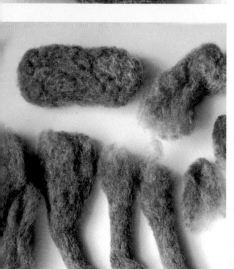

3 Form legs

Separate the 3rd and 4th fiber sections from Step 1 into halves; each half will be used to form a leg. Roll the fibers between your hands as you did to make the tail, but don't let it get too thin or pointy at the end. Refine the leg shape by needling and work 1 end into a round paw. The other end of each leg should be loose fiber. Shape the back legs further to include a bend in the knee.

4 Assemble kitty

Needle felt the legs onto the sides of the body and the tail to the back end. Use the fiber you set aside for the neck to form a bridge between the body and the head. Adjust the legs so they are even and the tail and head so they look natural. Continue shaping the cat until you are satisfied with its appearance. Needle felt eyes and a nose onto the face of the kitty with small bits of colored fiber.

Olde World Santa

Just a few details are all you need to give a needle-felted face its own personality. White locks for hair and a beard and a regal Christmas robe are all it takes to transform this sculpture into Santa. Making the center of the sculpture hollow saves on wool and makes this an easy-to-display decoration.

The project shown at left was made using Harrisville Designs Fleece in the following colors: 002 Red (A), 044 White (B), 042 Camel (C), 009 Evergreen (D), 030 Azure, 021 Violet and 050 Black.

FINISHED SIZE
22" × 6" × 5" (56cm × 15cm × 13cm)

MATERIALS
3⅛ oz. (87g) feltable wool fiber in 4 colors, 2 oz. (56g) of Fiber A, ¾ oz. (21g) of Fiber B, ¼ oz. (7g) of Fiber C and ⅛ oz. (3g) of Fiber D

1 oz. (28g) uncarded longwool locks

Small amounts of feltable wool fiber in several colors for embellishments

12" × 14" (30cm × 36cm) sheet of cardstock

30" × 14" (76cm × 36cm) piece of craft felt

Size 36 and 40 felting needles

Felting needle holder

Felting mat

Toothpick

Scissors

Stapler and staples

Straight pins

Pattern transfer supplies

White craft glue

1 Make head

Create a basic head sculpture using Fiber B as the base and Fiber C as the skintone of your choice (see *Step-by-Step Faces*, pages 116-120). Embellish the face with puffy eyebrows.

Using approximately ¼ oz. (7g) of Fiber A, form a cone shape on top of the head for a hat that is approximately 4" × 2½" (10cm × 6cm) after needle felting.

Separate the longwool locks, and choose 2–4 curls for the mustache. Attach the remaining locks around the head, just below the hat, and around the face for the beard. Attach the locks for the mustache to the center of the upper lip, trimming the locks shorter if necessary at the noncurling end before needle felting in place.

Embellish the hat by needle felting a ball of Fiber B at the tip and a brim covering both the edge of the hat and the top ends of the longwool locks.

2 Form body

Roll the cardstock into a loose cone with a 1½" (4cm) opening at the top and a 4" (10cm) opening at the bottom. Staple the cardstock to hold the cone shape. Trim each end of the cone flat.

Cut the craft felt into 2 pieces, 1 13" × 14" (33cm × 36cm) piece and 1 7" × 14" (18cm × 36cm) piece. Wrap the larger piece of felt around the cardstock cone. Trim the craft felt so that the edges overlap approximately 1" (3cm) and the felt extends about ½" (13mm) beyond the top and bottom edges of the cardstock. Set the cone aside.

Lay the trimmed craft felt flat on the felting mat. Cover 1 side with a layer of Fiber A. Needle felt the fiber into the craft felt, filling in open spaces as needed. Wrap the felt around the cardstock cone, it will have shrunken during felting and the edges will barely meet. Slide the smaller piece of craft felt under the opening between the edges. Pin the pieces of felt to the cone so the larger piece, or coat, is slightly open and some of the smaller piece is exposed. Trim the bottom and top edges of the smaller piece of felt to fit the cardstock cone. Slide the felt off of the cardstock. Slide the felting mat inside the coat and needle felt along the pinned area of the coat to attach the smaller piece of craft felt to the larger piece. Needle felt the pattern on page 151 to the exposed part of the smaller piece of craft felt.

3 Complete sculpture

Needle felt 4g of Fiber A into a cylinder approximately 1" × 6" (3cm × 15cm). Repeat for a 2nd arm. To make the mittens, use 1g of Fiber D for each mitten. Make a thumb by rolling a small cylinder with a toothpick, then needle felting. Needle felt the remaining portion of the wool to make a flat dome shape and attach the thumb to one side. Attach a mitten to the end of each arm.

Slide the coat onto the cardstock cone and pin the top of the arms to the side of the coat. Pin the sculpted head to the opening at the top of the coat. Look carefully at the sculpture and adjust the placement of any of the parts as needed. Slide the sculpture off of the cardstock cone and needle felt the coat to Santa's head and the arms to the coat. Once all of the pieces are firmly attached, glue the cone inside the coat.

Enlarge to 250% to bring to full size.

CHAPTER FOUR

Fulling Knitted & Crocheted Fabric

Knitted and crocheted items can be fulled to create a dense, fuzzy fabric. Fulling can transform a knitted or crocheted item into a much sturdier piece and is especially useful for items that need to be warm and hard-wearing, such as the Slipper Socks *on page 176,* or for items that need to be dense, such as the Reversible Striped Bag *on page 160,* to keep the items inside from slipping out. Stiffening a fulled fabric with hat-stiffening products adds a new dimension to your work because you can make a piece hold a specific shape, such as the Fedora Hat *on page 172.*

MATERIALS

Crocheted or knitted
  fabric

Cotton cord
  (optional)

Needle (optional)

Bowl or washtub

Hot water

Cold water

Dishwashing soap

Dry towel

Shaping tools
  (optional)

Hand Fulling, Step by Step

Hand fulling is the best technique to use with delicate
crocheted and knitted items, as well as if you want to be able
to monitor the progress of the fulling to achieve a certain size
or appearance.

1 Begin fulling

Prepare the edges of a piece if needed; the edges don't usually need to be prepared before hand fulling, though it can sometimes be helpful (see *Machine Fulling, Step by Step*, Step 1, page 157). Soak the project in a bowl of very warm to hot water with 1 teaspoon of dishwashing soap until it is fully saturated.

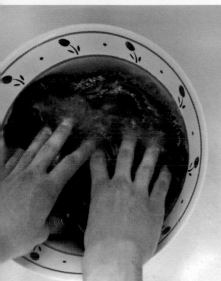

2 Full project

For hand fulling knitted and crocheted projects, you can use the *Flat Felting, Step by Step* method described on pages 42-47, or you can knead the project with your hands until it fulls. To full by hand, remove the project from the warm, soapy water and knead it with your hands. When it cools, wet the project in warm, soapy water. Then plunge it into cold water and knead it some more to help full the project completely.

When the piece is fulled the desired amount, run it through cool water to rinse out the soap. Squeeze out the excess water and roll the piece up in a dry towel to remove as much of the water as possible. Shape the piece into its finished shape and let it dry. If you plan to drastically change the shape of the piece, let it dry, then steam it with a steam iron and pull it into its finished shape or dry the piece on a form.

MATERIALS

Crocheted or knitted
  fabric
Cotton cord
  (optional)
Needle (optional)
Washing machine
Dishwashing soap
Jeans or other tough
  material (optional)
Shaping tools
  (optional)

Machine Fulling,
Step by Step

Knitted and crocheted fabrics can be fulled by machine.
Machine fulling is the faster, easier method, and most knitted
and crocheted pieces can stand up to the high agitation level
of machine fulling. However, the amount of fulling may be
dictated by the settings of your washing machine.

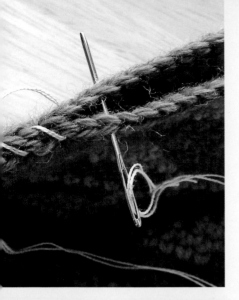

1 Prepare edges

Begin by preparing any exposed edges of the project so they won't stretch out of shape in the fulling process. Sometimes this is done during knitting or crocheting by working the last several rows in a nonfelting yarn, or by decreasing the last few rows so the outside edges are smaller than the rest of the piece. I often baste openings closed with a cotton cord.

2 First wash cycle

Place the item in the washing machine on the hot wash/cold rinse cycle at the lowest water level. Add 1–2 teaspoons of dishwashing soap. You can also add an old pair of jeans, or other tough material that will not fade, for extra agitation. Don't put anything in the washer with your project that can shed fibers, such as towels, because the shed fibers will get imbedded in the fabric. Start the washing machine.

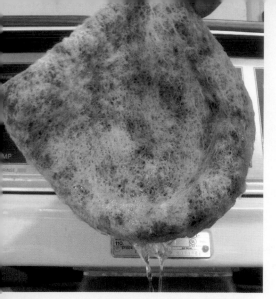

3 Check progress

Periodically stop the washer and take out your piece to see if it is fulled as much as you desire. In order to completely full an item, an entire machine cycle is usually needed. If the finished piece is meant to be worn, such as a hat or vest, check approximately every 5 minutes to make sure the piece doesn't full too small, or hasn't stretched out where it shouldn't.

4 Finish piece

When the piece has shrunk down to the size that you want, run it through the rinse and spin cycles, then remove any basting stitches. Shape the piece into its finished shape and let it dry. If you plan to drastically change the shape of the piece, let it dry, then steam it with a steam iron and pull it into its finished shape or dry the piece on a form.

Tips for Success

— Whenever a knitted or crocheted item that you will be fulling in the washing machine has an opening, be sure to decide ahead of time how you will keep the opening from flaring out during fulling. You must either decrease the last few rows or baste the opening closed if don't want the opening to stretch out of shape.

— If you want a drawstring closure on a project, you can knit or crochet the piece without adding holes, then string a shoelace through the stitches a few rows down from the top edge. Tie the ends of the shoelace together and throw the piece in the washer. This will eliminate the need to baste the openings or work holes into the pattern stitches.

— For a list of the abbreviations used in the knitting and crochet patterns, see the Glossary on pages 246-247.

Reversible Striped Bag

This colorful bag is a great introduction to fulled knitting because it's quick and easy and uses beautiful yarn. You are sure to have successful results whether this is your first fulled knitting project or your hundredth. An added bonus is that this bag looks just as good on the knit side as on the purl side, so wear it either way!

The project shown at left was made using Noro Kureyon (100% wool, 1¾ oz./50g, 110 yd./100m), 2 balls color #164, 1 ball color #132 and 1 ball color #134.

SKILL LEVEL
Beginner

FINISHED SIZE
Before fulling: Approx. 14½" (37cm) wide and 14" (36cm) tall when flat, not including handles

After fulling: Approx. 11½" (29cm) wide and 11" (28cm) tall when flat, not including handles

YARN
4 (1¾ oz./50g, 110 yd./100m) skeins feltable worsted weight variegated yarn: 2 in Color A, 1 each in colors that contrast with Color A (Colors B and C)

KNITTING NEEDLES
US 10½ (6.5mm) circular knitting needle, 29" (75cm) long

2 US 10½ (6.5mm) dpns

NOTIONS
Tapestry needle

Stitch marker

Pearl cotton

GAUGE
16 sts and 20 rows = 4" (10cm) in St st, before fulling

FULLING SUPPLIES
Washing machine

Dishwashing soap

Bag Body

With Color A and circular needle, CO 100 sts. Pm and join for working in the round. K 74 rnds, alternating 2 rnds A and 2 rnds B, replacing B with C when B is used up.

Bag Base

Continuing with A only, dec as foll:

RND 1: *K2, k2tog; rep from * to end—75 sts.

RND 2: Knit all sts.

RND 3: *K1, k2tog; rep from * to end—50 sts.

RND 4: Knit all sts.

RND 5: *K2tog; rep from * to end—25 sts.

RND 6: Knit all sts.

Cut yarn, leaving a 12" (30cm) tail. Thread tapestry needle with tail and pass through all rem sts, pulling them off the knitting needle as you pick them up with the tapestry needle. Pull the sts tight to close the opening. Pass the tail through the sts once more and fasten off. Weave in ends.

I-Cord Straps (make 2)

Using 2 dpns and yarn color of your choice, CO 7 sts, leaving a 12" (30cm) tail. K across the row. *Do not turn work, but keeping the RS facing you, slide the sts back to the right end of needle. Pull the working yarn across the back of the knitting and k across the row again. Repeat from * until knitting measures 12" (30cm). BO and cut yarn, leaving a 12" (30cm) tail.

Assembly

Using a tapestry needle and a 36" (91cm) length of yarn, roll the top edge of the bag to the RS and whipstitch in place, approximately 6 rows down from the edge.

Using the yarn tails on the Straps, sew the Straps to the top of the bag, placing the ends of the Straps about 4" (10cm) apart.

Fulling

Using the pearl cotton, baste the top of the bag closed. Throw the bag in the washer on the hot/cold setting and the lowest water level with some dishwashing soap (see *Machine Fulling, Step by Step*, pages 156-158). Check every 5–10 minutes to see if the fulling process is complete. When the bag is completely fulled, remove the basting, shape the bag, and let dry.

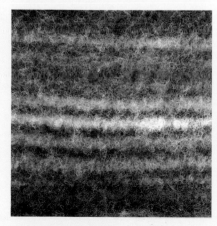

Knit side of fulled fabric

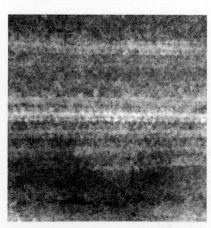

Purl side of fulled fabric

Twisted Handle Satchel

This single-strap bag boasts an easy opening with one side lower than the other so you can always get your hand into your bag, whether you are looking or not. The twisted I-cord handle is a great knitting technique that helps strengthen the rim of the bag while creating a wonderful textured handle.

The project shown at left was made using Brown Sheep Company Lamb's Pride Worsted (85% wool, 15% mohair, 4 oz./113g, 190 yd./174m) color M181 Prairie Fire.

SKILL LEVEL

Intermediate

FINISHED SIZE

Before fulling: Approx. 16" (41cm) wide and 20" (51cm) tall, not including handles
After fulling: Approx. 11" (28cm) wide and 12½" (32cm) tall, not including handles

YARN

3 (4 oz./113g, 190 yd./174m) skeins feltable worsted weight yarn

KNITTING NEEDLES

US 9 (5.5mm) circular knitting needle, 29" (75cm) long
Set of 5 US 9 (5.5mm) dpns

NOTIONS

Tapestry needle
Pearl cotton
Stitch markers
Stitch holders

GAUGE

16 sts and 22 rows = 4" (10cm) in St st, before fulling

FULLING SUPPLIES

Washing machine
Dishwashing soap

Bag Base

With dpns, leaving a 12" (30cm) tail, CO 18 sts, pm, CO 18 sts, pm—36 sts. Join for working in the round.

RNDS 1-24: *K to 1 st before m, kfb, sm, kfb; rep from * once more—132 sts.

Change to circular needle when necessary.

Bag Body

Work even in St st until piece measures 17" (43cm) from beg. End last rnd at either marker.

Shape top edge as foll:

ROW 1 (RS): K19, BO 28 sts, k around to bound-off sts. Leave markers in place. Turn work.

ROW 2 (WS): P2tog, p to last 2 sts, p2tog—2 sts dec.

ROW 3 (RS): K2tog, k to last 2 sts, k2tog—2 sts dec.

Rep Rows 2-3 8 times more, then Row 2 once more, until only the 66 sts on the back of the piece between the markers rem. BO rem sts.

Sew the bottom opening closed using the CO tail. Weave in ends.

Straps and Top Edge Trim

Using 2 dpns, with RS facing, pick up and k 4 sts along the right front edge of the top opening. Keeping the RS facing you, slide the sts from the left end of the needle to the right end. Bring the working yarn across the back of the needle and k4, then pick up and k another st from the edge of the bag. *Slide the sts to the right end of the needle and bring the yarn across the back again. K3, k2tog tbl, pick up and k 1 st from the edge of the bag. Repeat from * across front of bag, always working from right to left on RS of work, picking up 16 sts along each tapered side of the front and 20 sts along the 28 bound-off sts at center front. These ratios will draw in the opening so that it will not flare out when fulled. When you reach the opposite side of the bag, work 4-st I-cord for 25" (64cm). Place sts on holder and cut yarn leaving a 12" (30cm) tail.

Pick up and k 4 sts from the right back edge of top opening and work applied I-cord across the back of the bag as for front, picking up 46 sts along back edge. When you reach the opposite side of the bag, work 25" (64cm) of 4-st I-cord. Place sts on holder and cut yarn leaving a 12" (30cm) tail.

Twist the I-cords around each other several times. Use the tails to graft the ends of the cords to the first row of each applied I-cord edge.

Fulling

Arrange the twisted handle so that the twists are evenly spaced along the strap. Using the pearl cotton, tie the 2 strands of I-cord together at each twist with a square knot to hold them securely in place. Throw the bag in the washer on the hot/cold setting and the lowest water level with some dishwashing soap. Check every 5–10 minutes to see if the fulling process is complete. When the bag is completely fulled, remove the ties, shape the bag and let it dry.

Sock Knitting Needle Roll

I like to use fulled projects for holding my needlework tools because the dense finished fabric is strong and durable and helps protect my tools. This little case for double-pointed knitting needles is small enough to stash in a purse, yet it holds several sets of needles.

The project shown at left was made using Araucania Atacama (100% alpaca, 1¾ oz./50g, 110 yd./100m), color 522.

SKILL LEVEL

Intermediate

FINISHED SIZE

Before fulling: Approx. 13" (33cm) wide by 10½" (27cm) tall
After fulling: Approx. 9" (23cm) wide by 8" (20cm) tall

YARN

1 (1¾ oz./50g, 110 yd./100m) skein feltable DK weight yarn

KNITTING NEEDLES

US 4 (3.5mm) straight knitting needles

NOTIONS

12" (30cm) piece of 44" (1.1m) fabric for lining, or 1 fat quarter
12" (30cm) single-fold bias tape
Tapestry needle
Straight pins
Steam iron
Sewing machine
Sewing thread to match fabric
¾" (2cm) button

GAUGE

23 sts and 29 rows = 4" (10cm) in St st, before fulling

FULLING SUPPLIES

Bubble wrap
Hot, soapy water
Dowel rod
Rubberbands

Case

CO 60 sts. Work in St st until piece measures 13" (33cm). BO. Weave in ends.

Fulling

Steam block the knitted rectangle so it lies flat. Full the knitted fabric (see *Flat Felting, Step by Step*, pages 42-47). When the piece is fulled, rinse out the soapy water and lay the piece flat to dry. When the piece is dry, fold it in thirds and steam press to set the folds.

Lining

Cut a piece of fabric for the lining to measure ½" (1cm) larger than the fulled rectangle on all sides.

Cut a second piece of fabric for the pocket to measure 12" (30cm) long and the same width as the lining. Fold the pocket in half lengthwise and press. Fold the bias tape over the folded edge of the pocket and topstitch.

Lay the pocket RS up on the RS of the lining, matching raw edges, and pin in place. Make channels for sock needles by sewing through all layers, spacing the lines of stitching ½" (1cm) apart, or more for larger size needles.

Turn under all raw edges ½" (1cm) and press. Lay the lining on top of the fulled rectangle and stitch in place around the edges and along the fold lines in the fulled fabric.

Sew a button on one of the short edges. Make a button loop with thread opposite the button.

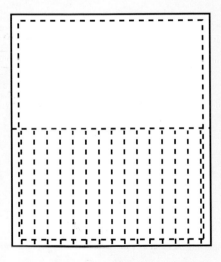

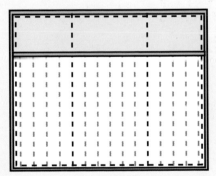

Fedora Hat

Making a fulled hat is exciting when you find out that you can make it look just like a professionally made hat. One tip for making this hat is to take the time to full the fabric completely. But the real secret is to use a hat form and water-based shellac to get the finished hat to be the same shape and stiffness as a hat you would buy at a hat store.

The project shown at left was made using Harrisville Designs New England Highland (100% wool, 3½ oz./100g, 200 yd./183m), color 039 Russet.

SKILL LEVEL
Intermediate

FINISHED SIZE
Crown circumference:
  22" (56cm)
Brim circumference:
  34" (86cm)

YARN
1 (3½ oz./100g, 200 yd./183m) skein feltable worsted weight yarn

KNITTING NEEDLES
US 9 (5.5mm) circular knitting needle, 24" (60cm) long
Set of 4 US 9 (5.5mm) dpns

NOTIONS
Tapestry needle
Stitch markers
Grosgrain ribbon
Double-fold bias binding
Stabilizer
Small feathers (optional)
White craft glue (optional)

GAUGE
16 sts and 22 rows = 4" (10cm) in St st, before fulling

FULLING SUPPLIES
Hot, soapy water
Hat form
Steam iron
Wooden mallet
Water-based shellac

Crown

With dpns, CO 6 sts and join for working in the round.

RND 1: Knit all sts.

RND 2: *Kfb; rep from * to end—12 sts.

RND 3: Knit all sts.

RND 4: *Pm, kfb, k1; rep from * to end—18 sts, 6 markers.

RND 5: Knit all sts.

RND 6: *Sm, kfb, k2; rep from * to end—24 sts.

RND 7: Knit all sts.

RND 8: *Sm, kfb, k to next m; rep from * to end—30 sts.

Rep Rnds 7–8 10 times more—90 sts.

Narrow Brim

Work 25 rnds even.

NEXT RND: *Sm, kfb, k to next m; rep from * to end—96 sts.

NEXT RND: Knit all sts.

Rep last 2 rnds 6 times more—132 sts.

BO.

Weave in ends.

Wide Brim Variation

Work 35 rnds even.

NEXT RND: *Sm, kfb, k to next m; rep from * to end—96 sts.

NEXT RND: Knit all sts.

Rep last 2 rnds 9 times more—150 sts.

BO.

Weave in ends.

Fulling

Hand full the hat in a sinkful of hot, soapy water until it begins to shrink (see *Hand Fulling, Step by Step*, pages 154-155). Check the hat on the hat form occasionally for size and continue fulling until the hat fits snugly on the form. Rinse the soap out with warm water, and squeeze as much water out of the hat as possible. Using the steam iron, heat the hat, then shape it on the hat form, pounding the surface with a wooden mallet to get a smooth, tight-fitting shape. Let the hat dry on the form. When the hat is completely dry, apply the water-based shellac following the manufacturer's instructions.

Assembly

Pin a strip of stabilizer to the inside edge of the hat just above the brim, and adjust it so that the hat is the desired size; trim the ends so they overlap approximately ½" (1cm). Stitch the stabilizer to the bottom edge of the hat, along the fold. Cover the stabilizer with double-fold bias binding and sew in place. Cut a 22" (56cm) strip of grosgrain ribbon and steam press it so that one edge is longer than the other, creating a gentle curve. Place the ribbon on the outside of the hat and adjust it until it fits snugly around the brim of the hat, with the raw edges meeting on the left side of the hat. Pin the ribbon in place. If desired, create a bow with an additional piece of ribbon. Pin the bow over the raw edges of the ribbon on the brim of the hat. Adjust the ribbons so they are even and snug and the raw edges of the ribbon are covered by the bow. Sew the ribbon in place along the brim of the hat and tack the bow edges in place. If desired, slide one or more feathers behind the bow. If they don't fit snuggly, use a small amount of glue to adhere them behind the bow.

Slipper Socks

These comfy, cozy socks make the most of washable wool and feltable wool. You knit them with both types of yarn, then throw them in the washer and let the feltable wool full into a warm, fuzzy sole, while the washable wool cuff stays soft and stretchy.

The projects shown at left were made using Brown Sheep Company Wildfoote (75% washable wool, 25% nylon, 1¾ oz./50g, 215 yd./197m), color SY-600 Symphony (A) and Brown Sheep Company Lamb's Pride Worsted (85% wool, 15% mohair, 4 oz./113g, 190 yd./174m), color #M270 Royal Purple Flutter (B).

SKILL LEVEL

Intermediate

FINISHED SIZE

Before fulling: Approx. 12" (30cm) long and 9½" (24cm) in circumference (unstretched)

After fulling: Approx. 9½" (24cm) long and 6½" (17cm) in circumference (unstretched)

YARN

1 (1¾ oz./50g, 215 yd./197m) skein of nonfelting sock weight yarn (A)

1 (4 oz./113g, 190 yd./174m) skein of feltable worsted weight yarn (B)

KNITTING NEEDLES

Set of 4 US 4 (3.5mm) dpns

Set of 4 US 6 (4mm) dpns

Set of 4 US 8 (5mm) dpns

NOTIONS

Tapestry needle

Stitch markers

Stitch holders

No-slip slipper bottoms (optional)

GAUGE

19 sts and 26 rows = 4" (10cm) in St st using US 8 (5mm) needles and worsted weight yarn, before fulling

FULLING SUPPLIES

Washing machine

Dishwashing soap

Stitch Instructions

2 × 2 Rib (multiple of 4 sts):
*Every rnd: *P2, k2; rep from * to end.*

Work 2 tog:
K2tog or p2tog to match est st patt.

Work even:
K on RS, P on WS.

Cuff

With 2 strands of Yarn A held together and US 6 (4mm) dpns, CO 44 sts. Join for working in the round. Change to US 4 (3.5mm) dpns and work 10 rnds in St st. Work in 2 × 2 Rib for 3" (8cm).

Instep

Place first 18 sts of rnd on a holder. Work back and forth in est rib patt over rem 26 sts for 6" (15cm), ending with a WS row.

DEC ROW (RS): Work 2 tog, work in est rib patt to last 2 sts, work 2 tog—2 sts dec.

NEXT ROW (WS): Work in est patt.

Rep last 2 rows 4 times more—16 sts.

Place rem sts on a second holder.

Sole

Using Yarn B and US 8 (5mm) dpns, with RS facing, pick up and k 1 st from the edge of the Instep just before the 18 sts on the first st holder, k 18 sts from holder, and pick up and k 1 st from the other side of the Instep—20 sts.

Continue working flat.

ROW 1 (WS): Sl 1, p to end, pick up and p 1 st from the side of the heel flap—21 sts.

ROW 2 (RS): Sl 1, k to end, pick up and k 1 st from the side of the heel flap—22 sts.

Rep Rows 1–2 3 times more—28 sts.

The remainder of the Sole is worked in the round.

With RS facing, pick up and k 22 sts from the side of the Instep, k 16 sts from the second holder, and pick up and k 22 sts from the opposite side of the Instep—88 sts. K to the center back of the heel and pm for beg of rnd.

RND 1: K19, (k1, kfb) 6 times, k26, (k1, kfb) 6 times, k19—100 sts.

RNDS 2–6: Knit all sts.

RND 7: K5, k2tog, k28, (k2tog, k4) 2 times, k2tog, k2, k2tog, (k4, k2tog) 2 times, k28, k2tog, k5—92 sts.

RND 8: Knit all sts.

RND 9: K5, k2tog, k26, (k2tog, k3) 2 times, k2tog, k2, k2tog, (k3, k2tog) 2 times, k26, k2tog, k5—84 sts.

RND 10: Knit all sts.

RND 11: K5, k2tog, k24, (k2tog, k2) twice, k2tog, k2, k2tog, (k2, k2tog) 2 times, k24, k2tog, k5—76 sts.

RND 12: Knit all sts.

RND 13: K5, k2tog, k22, (k2tog, k1) 3 times, (k1, k2tog) 3 times, k22, k2tog, k5—68 sts.

RND 14: Knit all sts.

RND 15: (K1, k2tog) 3 times, k19, (k2tog) 6 times, k19, (k2tog, k1) 3 times—56 sts.

Divide rem sts in half and graft halves together along center bottom of foot.

Fulling

Wash the slipper socks in the washer on the hot/cold setting and the lowest water level with some dishwashing soap (see *Machine Fulling, Step by Step*, pages 156-158). Check every 5–10 minutes for size and fit as well as degree of fulling. When the socks have fulled to the desired size, shape them and allow them to dry completely.

If desired, attach no-slip slipper bottoms to the soles of the slipper socks. The fulled fabric can be quite slippery on wood or tile, so consider where the wearer will be walking and attach no-slip slipper bottoms for safety if necessary.

Decorative Rose

Knitted and fulled roses and leaves
are wonderful accents to add to many
items, from bags to blankets. This rose
is knitted in pieces, sewn together at
the base, then thrown in the washer
with the leaves until it becomes nice
and fuzzy all over. Use it as a pin, or a
decorative element on another project.

*The project shown at left was made
using Noro Kureyon (100% wool, 1¾
oz./50g, 110 yd./100m) color #154.*

SKILL LEVEL

Beginner

FINISHED SIZE

Before fulling: Approx.
   6" (15cm) across
After fulling: Approx.
   4" (10cm) across

YARN

1 (1¾ oz./50g,
   110 yd./100m)
   skein variegated
   single-ply feltable
   worsted weight yarn
   containing your
   desired colors OR
   1 skein single-ply
   worsted weight
   yarn in each of your
   desired colors

KNITTING NEEDLES

US 8 (5mm) straight
   needles

NOTIONS

Tapestry needle

GAUGE

19 sts and 26 rows =
   4" (10cm) in St st,
   before fulling

FULLING SUPPLIES

Washing machine
Dishwashing soap

Stitch Instructions

SKP:
Sl 1 st as if to knit, k1, pass slipped st over.

S2KP:
Sl 2 sts kwise at the same time, k1, pass 2 slipped sts over.

Leaves (make 2)

CO 3 sts with color of your choice. (If using variegated yarn, begin with the color you want at the base of the leaf.)

ROW 1 (RS): K1, yo, k1, yo, k1—5 sts.

ROW 2 and all WS rows: Purl all sts.

ROW 3: K2, yo, k1, yo, k2—7 sts.

ROW 5: K3, yo, k1, yo, k3—9 sts.

ROW 7: K4, yo, k1, yo, k4—11 sts.

ROW 9: K5, yo, k1, yo, k5—13 sts.

ROW 11: K6, yo, k1, yo, k6—15 sts.

ROW 13: Knit all sts.

ROW 15: K6, S2KP, k6—13 sts.

ROW 17: K5, S2KP, k5—11 sts.

ROW 19: K4, S2KP, k4—9 sts.

ROW 21: K3, S2KP, k3—7 sts.

ROW 23: K2, S2KP, k2—5 sts.

ROW 25: K1, S2KP, k1—3 sts.

Cut yarn leaving a 3" (8cm) tail, pull through rem sts and fasten off. Weave in ends.

Flower Center (make 1)

CO 35 sts with the color of your choice. (If using variegated yarn, begin with the color you want at the center base of the flower.)

ROW 1 (RS): K to last 2 sts, k2tog—34 sts.

ROW 2 (WS): Purl all sts.

Rep last 2 rows 6 times more—28 sts.

BO and cut yarn, leaving an 8" (20cm) tail. Do not weave in ends.

Petals (make 4)

CO 20 sts with the color of your choice. (If using variegated yarn, begin with the color you want at the base of the petal.)

ROWS 1–6: Work in St st beg with a k row.

ROW 7 (RS): SKP, k to last 2 sts, k2tog—18 sts.

ROW 8: Purl all sts.

ROW 9: SKP, k to last 2 sts, k2tog—16 sts.

ROW 10: P2tog, p to last 2 sts, p2tog—14 sts.

ROW 11: SKP, k to last 2 sts, k2tog—12 sts.

ROW 12: P2tog, BO each st across until 2 sts rem, p2tog.

BO and cut yarn, leaving an 8" (20cm) tail. Do not weave in ends.

Assembly

Using the tails from the petals and flower center, sew the pieces together with a tapestry needle. First, roll the flower center into a tight spiral and secure it at the base. Then tack each petal around the center, overlapping petals by 1" (3cm) or more. Tack the leaves to the bottom of the flower. Weave in all yarn ends.

Fulling

Throw in the washer on the hot/cold setting and the lowest water level with some dishwashing soap (see *Machine Fulling, Step by Step*, pages 156-158). Check every 5–10 minutes to see if the fulling process is complete. When the flower is completely fulled, shape it and let it dry completely.

Colorwork Bag

Fulling a colorwork project can create a beautiful fabric that blends the image into a more subtle design than if left unfulled. I've combined a simple design with a detailed pattern to create a bag with rich design changes. The subtle color-changing yarn adds to the movement of the patterns.

The project shown at left was made using Knit One Crochet Too Paint Box (100% wool, 1¾ oz./50g, 100 yd./91m), colors 11 and 01.

SKILL LEVEL

Intermediate

FINISHED SIZE

Before fulling: Approx. 20" (51cm) wide and 23" (58cm) tall, when flat

After fulling: Approx. 19" (48cm) wide and 19" (48cm) tall, when flat

YARN

8 (1¾ oz./50g, 100 yd./91m) skeins variegated single-ply feltable worsted weight yarn, 4 skeins each in a light colorway and a dark colorway

KNITTING NEEDLES

US 9 (5.5mm) circular knitting needle, 29" (74cm) long

NOTIONS

Tapestry needle
Stitch marker
2 leather handles
8 decorative buttons

GAUGE

19 sts and 26 rows = 4" (10cm) in St st, before fulling

FULLING SUPPLIES

Bubble wrap
Hot, soapy water
Dowel rod
Rubberbands

Body

With darker yarn, CO 192 sts, pm and join for working in the round.
Work Chart 2. Rep Rnd 1 of Chart 1 25 times, then complete Chart 1 through Rnd 32.
Work Chart 2.
BO.

Base

Using one strand each of darker and lighter yarns held together, with RS facing, pick up and k 20 sts from the CO of the Body. Work back and forth in garter st for 120 rows. BO.

Assembly

Sew the 3 unattached sides of the Base to the Body.

Fulling

Full the knitted fabric (see *Flat Felting, Step by Step*, pages 42-47). When the piece is fulled, rinse out the soapy water. Shape the bag and allow it to dry completely. Sew the handles and buttons to the bag.

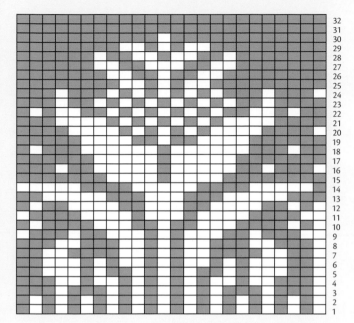

Chart 1

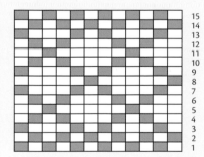

Chart 2

Colorwork Coin Purse

This little coin purse is made using colorwork crochet. A nice feature to colorwork projects made using crochet is that there are no floating strands of yarn on the back of the work as there is in knitting. This is because you hold the yarn you are not using along the top of the row and crochet it into each stitch as you work.

The project shown at left was made using Cascade Yarns Cascade 220 (100% wool, 3½ oz./100g, 220 yd./200m), colors 9447 (A) and 9407 (B).

SKILL LEVEL

Intermediate

FINISHED SIZE

Before fulling: 6" × 6" (15cm × 15cm)

After fulling: 5½" × 4¼" (14cm × 11cm)

YARN

2 (3½ oz./100g, 220 yd./200m) skeins feltable worsted weight yarn, 1 each in 2 colors (A and B)

HOOK

US H (5mm) crochet hook

NOTIONS

Tapestry needle

Pearl cotton

7" (18cm) zipper

Sewing needle and thread to match darker yarn

Straight pins

9" (23cm) decorative trim (optional)

GAUGE

16 sc and 20 rows = 4" (10cm), before fulling

FULLING SUPPLIES

Washing machine

Dishwashing soap

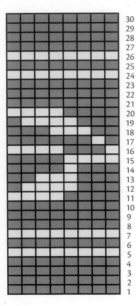

30
29
28
27
26
25
24
23
22
21
20
19
18
17
16
15
14
13
12
11
10
9
8
7
6
5
4
3
2
1

Purse

With yarn A, ch 24.

ROW 1: Sc in the back half of second ch from hook and each ch to last ch, 3 sc in last ch. Rotate work and sc in other side of each ch, ending with 2 sc in last ch. Join with sl st to first sc—48 sts.

Follow the 8-st repeat of the chart at left for the remainder of purse, crocheting over the color not in use. Join with sl st at beg of each rnd. Always begin a color change by pulling the new color through the last half of the stitch before the color change.

Fasten off and weave in ends.

Fulling

Using the pearl cotton and tapestry needle, baste the opening of the purse closed. Throw in the washer on the hot/cold setting and the lowest water level with some dishwashing soap (see *Machine Fulling, Step by Step*, pages 156-158). Check every 5–10 minutes to see if the fulling process is complete. When the purse is completely fulled, shape it and let it dry completely.

Finishing

To add a zipper to the purse opening, cut the zipper to approximately ¼" (6mm) longer than the purse opening. Using the sewing needle and thread, stitch over the zipper teeth at the cut end to secure. Pin the zipper to the inside of the purse and hand sew in place. Overcast the edges of the zipper to the inside of the purse for a neat finish, or sew a decorative trim over the zipper edges.

Crochet Hook Case

Here's a perfect holder for all of your favorite crochet hooks. Just like the *Sock Knitting Needle Roll* on page 168, this is a flat piece of work that is used for the outside of a lined, pocketed folder. The crocheting is fulled and hardened until it becomes a strong cover for protecting and storing your tools.

The project shown at left was made using Araucania Atacama (100% alpaca, 1¾ oz./50g, 110 yd./100m), color 402.

SKILL LEVEL
Intermediate

FINISHED SIZE
Before fulling:
  Approximately 10½"
  (27cm) across
After fulling:
  Approximately 8"
  (20cm) across

YARN
1 (1¾ oz./50g, 110 yd./100m) skein felt-able DK weight yarn

HOOK
US G (4mm) crochet hook

NOTIONS
Tapestry needle
Removable marker
12" (30cm) piece of 44" (1.1m) fabric for lining, or 1 fat quarter
12" (30cm) single-fold bias tape
Sewing machine
Sewing thread to match fabric
Magnetic snap

GAUGE
20 sc and 22 rows – 4" (10cm), before fulling

FULLING SUPPLIES
Bubble wrap
Hot, soapy water
Dowel rod
Rubberbands
Steam iron

Case
Ch 2.

RND 1: 6 sc in 2nd ch from hook. Do not turn.

RND 2: Cont in the round, work 2 sc in each sc around, pm in last st—12 sts.

RND 3: (Sc in next st, 2 sc in next st) 6 times, move marker to last st—18 sts.

RND 4: (Sc in next 2 sts, 2 sc in next st) 6 times, move marker to last st—24 sts.

RND 5: (Sc in next 3 sts, 2 sc in next st) 6 times, move marker to last st—30 sts.

RND 6: (Sc in next 4 sts, 2 sc in next st) 6 times, move marker to last st—36 sts.

Cont as set, working incs at 6 points every rnd, until you have 174 sts—29 rnds total.

Fasten off and weave in ends.

Fulling
Full the crocheted fabric (see *Flat Felting, Step by Step*, pages 42-47). When the piece is fulled, rinse out the soapy water and lay the piece flat to dry. When the piece is dry, fold it in half and steam press to set the fold.

Lining

Cut the fabric for the lining to ½" (13mm) larger than the fulled hexagon on all sides. Cut fabric for the pocket to 11" (28cm) long and equal in width to the lining. Fold the pocket fabric in half lengthwise and press. Fold the bias tape over the folded edge of the pocket and topstitch.

Lay the pocket RS up on the RS of the lining, matching raw edges, and pin in place. Make channels for crochet hooks by sewing through all layers, spacing the lines of stitching ⅜" (1cm) apart.

Turn under all raw edges ½" (1cm) and press. Lay lining on top of fulled hexagon and stitch in place around the edge and down the center fold line. Attach the magnetic snap following the manufacturer's instructions.

Bowl with Handles

This small bowl starts simply, but ends with an openwork pattern along the top rows for a decorative touch. I made this project into a bowl, but I didn't use any stiffening products, so it is still soft and pliable. Because of this, the project could also double as a bag.

The project shown at left was made using Mountain Colors 4/8's Wool (100% wool, 3½ oz./100g, 250 yd./229m), Flathead Cherry.

SKILL LEVEL

Intermediate

FINISHED SIZE

Before fulling: Base diameter approx. 9" (23cm), height approx. 6½" (17cm)
After fulling: Base diameter approx. 7" (18cm), height approx. 5" (13cm)

YARN

1 (3½ oz./100g, 250 yd./229m) skein of variegated feltable worsted weight yarn

HOOK

US H (5mm) crochet hook

NOTIONS

Tapestry needle
Pearl cotton
Removable marker

GAUGE

20 sc and 22 rows = 4" (10cm) before fulling

FULLING SUPPLIES

Washing machine
Dishwashing soap

Bowl Base and Sides

Ch 2.

RND 1: 6 sc in 2nd ch from hook. Do not turn.

RND 2: Cont in the rnd, work 2 sc in each st around, pm in last st—12 sts.

RND 3: (Sc in next st, 2 sc in next st) 6 times, move marker to last st—18 sts.

RND 4: (Sc in next 2 sts, 2 sc in next st) 6 times, move marker to last st—24 sts.

RND 5: (Sc in next 3 sts, 2 sc in next st) 6 times, move marker to last st—30 sts.

RND 6: (Sc in next 4 sts, 2 sc in next st) 6 times, move marker to last st—36 sts.

Cont as set, working incs at 6 points every rnd, until you have 102 sts—17 rnds total.

NEXT RND: (Sc in next 50 sc, 2 sc in next sc) 2 times, move marker to last st—104 sts.

Work 16 rnds even.

Top of Bowl and Handles

RND 1: Ch 3 (counts as 1 dc), *dc in next 2 sts, (ch 1, sk 1 st, dc in next st) 3 times; rep from * 11 times more, dc in next 2 sts, (ch 1, sk 1 st, dc in next st) 2 times, ch 1, sk 1 st, join with sl st in top of beg ch-3.

RND 2: Sl st in first dc, *(3 dc, ch 1, 3 dc) in 2nd ch-1 sp, sk next 2 dc, sc in next dc; rep from * 11 times more, (3 dc, ch 1, 3 dc) in 2nd ch-1 sp, sk next 2 dc, sc in beg sl st to join—13 shells.

RND 3: Ch 5, *sc in top of next shell, ch 2, 1 dc in next sc, ch 2; rep from * 12 times more, join with sl st in 3rd ch of beg ch-5.

RND 4: Ch 3, dc in each st and ch around, join with sl st in top of beg ch-3—78 sts.

RND 5: *Ch 15, sk 15 sts, sc in next 24 sts; rep from * once, sl st in first ch to join.

RNDS 6-7: Sc in each st and ch around, sl st in first sc to join. Fasten off and weave in ends.

Fulling

Baste the opening of the bowl shut with pearl cotton. Throw in the washer on the hot/cold setting and lowest water level with some dishwashing soap. Check every 5–10 minutes to see if the fulling process is complete. When the bowl is completely fulled, remove the basting, shape the bowl and let it dry.

Zippered Vest

The trick to successfully fulling a gar-
ment is to use the gauge measurements
from a fulled test swatch. That way, you
will be making measurement decisions
based on the fulled stitch size instead
of estimating shrinkage rates. The edges
on this vest are worked in a washable
wool, so that they will not change size
during the fulling process. This keeps
the edges of the vest firm with a clean
edge, making the jacket an easy project
to work and finish.

*The project shown at left was made
using Brown Sheep Company Lamb's
Pride Worsted (85% wool, 15% mohair, 4
oz./113g, 190 yd./174m), color M07 (MC),
and Brown Sheep Company Wildfoote
(75% superwash wool, 25% nylon, 1¾
oz./50g, 215 yd./197m), color SY05 (CC).*

SKILL LEVEL

Intermediate

FINISHED SIZE

Bust: 40" (102cm),
    after fulling
Length: 25" (64cm),
    after fulling

YARN

6 (4 oz./113g, 190
    yd./174m) skeins
    single-ply feltable
    worsted weight yarn
    (MC)
4 (1¾ oz./50g, 215
    yd./197m) skeins
    nonfelting sock
    weight yarn (CC)

HOOKS

US I (5.5mm) crochet
    hook
US E (3.5mm) crochet
    hook

NOTIONS

Tapestry needle
Removable stitch
    markers
Sewing needle and
    thread
Straight pins
20" (51cm) separating
    zipper

GAUGE

10½ pattern repeats
    and 10 rows = 4"
    (10cm) after fulling

FULLING
SUPPLIES

Washing machine
Dishwashing soap
Dryer (optional)

Lower Body

With larger hook and MC, ch 204.

ROW 1: Dc in 6th ch from hook, *ch 1, sk 1, dc in next ch; rep from * to end—100 pattern reps.

ROWS 2–32: Ch 4 (counts as dc, ch 1 here and throughout), dc in 1st ch-1 sp, *ch 1, dc in next ch-1 sp; rep from * to end. Mark the 6 pattern reps around each side "seam" for the base of the armholes. To do this, count in 25 pattern reps from each edge; this is the side seamline. Count 3 reps to the side of each side seamline and place markers.

Right Front

ROW 33 (RS): Ch 4, dc in 1st ch-1 sp, *ch 1, dc in next ch-1 sp; rep from * to last patt rep before armhole marker, dc in last ch-1 sp—21 patt reps.

ROW 34 (WS): Ch 3 (counts as dc here and throughout), dc in 1st ch-1 sp, *ch 1, dc in next ch-1 sp; rep from * to end—20 patt reps.

ROW 35: Ch 4, dc in 1st ch-1 sp, *ch 1, dc in next ch-1 sp; rep from * to last patt rep, sk next ch-1 sp, dc in next dc—19 patt reps.

ROW 36: Ch 4, dc in 1st ch-1 sp, *ch 1, dc in next ch-1 sp; rep from * to last patt rep, dc in last ch-1 sp—18 patt reps.

ROWS 37, 39, 41, 43, 45, 47, 49, 51 (RS): Ch 3, dc in 1st ch-1 sp, *ch 1, dc in next ch-1 sp; rep from * to end—10 patt reps.

ROWS 38, 40, 42, 44, 46, 48, 50, 52 (WS): Ch 4, dc in 1st ch-1 sp, *ch 1, dc in next ch-1 sp; rep from * to last patt rep, sk next ch-1 sp, ch 1, dc in next dc.

ROWS 53–59: Ch 4, dc in 1st ch-1 sp, *ch 1, dc in next ch-1 sp; rep from * to end.

Fasten off.

Back

Join yarn in 1st dc after marked armhole base with RS facing.

ROW 33 (RS): Ch 3, dc in 1st ch-1 sp, *ch 1, dc in next ch-1 sp; rep from * to last patt rep before marker, dc in last ch-1 sp—42 patt reps.

ROWS 34–35: Ch 3, dc in 1st ch-1 sp, *ch 1, dc in next ch-1 sp; rep from * to last patt rep, sk next ch-1 sp, dc in next dc—38 patt reps.

ROW 36: Ch 4, dc in 1st ch-1 sp, *ch 1, dc in next ch-1 sp; rep from * to last patt rep, sk next ch-1 sp, ch 1, dc in next dc—38 patt reps.

ROWS 37–57: Ch 4, dc in 1st ch-1 sp, *ch 1, dc in next ch-1 sp; rep from * to end.

Left shoulder:

ROW 58 (WS): Ch 4, dc in 1st ch-1 sp, (ch 1, dc in next ch-1 sp) ten times. Turn.

ROW 59: Ch 3, dc in 1st ch-1 sp, *ch 1, dc in next ch-1 sp; rep from * to end.

Fasten off.

Right shoulder:

With WS facing, count back 11 patt reps from armhole edge and join yarn in preceding dc.

ROW 58 (WS): Ch 4, dc in 1st ch-1 sp, *ch 1, dc in next ch-1 sp; rep from * to end.

ROW 59: Ch 4, dc in 1st ch-1 sp, *ch 1, dc in next ch-1 sp; rep from * to last patt rep, dc in last ch-1 sp.

Fasten off.

Left Front

Join yarn in 1st dc after marked armhole base with RS facing.

ROW 33 (RS): Ch 3, dc in 1st ch-1 sp, *ch 1, dc in next ch-1 sp; rep from * to end—21 patt reps.

ROW 34 (WS): Ch 4, dc in 1st ch-1 sp, *ch 1, dc in next ch-1 sp; rep from * to last patt rep, sk next ch-1 sp, dc in next dc—20 patt reps.

ROW 35: Rep Row 33—19 patt reps.

ROW 36: Ch 3, dc in 1st ch-1 sp, *ch 1, dc in next ch-1 sp; rep from * to last patt rep, sk next ch-1 sp, ch 1, dc in last dc—18 patt reps.

ROWS 37, 39, 41, 43, 45, 47, 49, 51 (RS): Ch 4, dc in 1st ch-1 sp, *ch 1, dc in next ch-1 sp; rep from * to last patt rep, sk next ch-1 sp, dc in last dc—10 patt reps.

ROWS 38, 40, 42, 44, 46, 48, 50 (WS): Ch 4, dc in 1st ch-1 sp, *ch 1, dc in next ch-1 sp; rep from * to end.

ROWS 52–59: Ch 4, dc in 1st ch-1 sp, *ch 1, dc in next ch-1 sp; rep from * to end.

Fasten off.

Seam shoulders.

Edging

With smaller hook and 2 strands of CC held together, join yarn anywhere along edge of vest. Work 2 sc in each ch-sp and row around edge. To round corners, work (2 sc, ch 2, 2 sc) in 1 st. When you have worked all around edge of vest, join with sl st in 1st sc, ch 1, and work a second row of sc, working 1 sc in each sc of previous row. The edging will be much tighter than the body fabric; this will cinch in the body around the edges so it won't flare out during fulling.

Repeat edging around each armhole.

Fulling

Throw the vest in the washer on the lowest water setting and a hot/cold cycle. Check it occasionally to see that it is fulling and not stretching out of shape. When it has fulled to the correct size, remove from the washer, pull into the finished shape and allow it to dry completely. You can also put it in the dryer if you want it to full a little more.

Finishing

Pin the zipper in place behind the edging of each side of the front opening and hand sew in place.

Openwork Rug

This rug is a great example of an interesting way to combine fulling and crochet. Because it is so easy to make motifs in crochet, and because they maintain their shape and texture when fulled, you can create this openwork design easily with recognizable shapes.

The project shown at left was made using Harrisville Designs New England Highland (100% wool, 3½ oz./100g, 200 yd./183m) in colors 040 Topaz (A), 039 Russet (B), 008 Hemlock (C), 004 Gold (D), 036 Garnet (E), 007 Tundra (F), 068 Olive (G) and 065 Poppy (H).

SKILL LEVEL
Intermediate

FINISHED SIZE
Approximately 30" × 25" (76cm × 64cm)

YARN
11 (3½ oz./100g, 200 yd./183m) skeins of feltable worsted weight yarn, 2 skeins each in 3 colors (A, B and C), and 1 skein each in 5 colors (D, E, F, G and H)

HOOK
US H (5mm) crochet hook

NOTIONS
Tapestry needle

GAUGE
16 sc and 8 rows = 4" (10cm)

FULLING SUPPLIES
Pearl cotton
1 yd. (.9m) nylon netting
Nylon stocking
Dryer
2 tennis balls
Boiling water

Stitch Instructions

dc2tog:
(Yo, pull up a loop in next st, yo, pull through 2 loops on hook) twice, yo, pull through all loops on hook.

Elm Leaf

(Make1 each in Yarns A, B, D, E, F and G.)

Ch 4.

ROW 1: 3 dc in 4th ch from hook. Turn.

ROW 2: Ch 3, dc in next 3 dc, 2 dc in top of ch-3. Turn—6 sts.

ROW 3: Ch 3, dc in next 5 dc, 2 dc in top of ch-3. Turn—8 sts.

ROWS 4–6: Ch 3, sk 1st dc, dc in next 6 dc, dc in top of ch-3. Turn—8 sts.

ROW 7: Ch 3, sk 1st dc, dc in next 6 dc. Turn—7 sts.

ROW 8: Ch 3, sk 1st dc, dc in next 5 dc. Turn—6 sts.

ROW 9: Ch 3, sk 1st dc, dc in next 4 dc. Turn—5 sts.

ROW 10: Ch 3, sk 1st dc, dc in next 3 dc.—4 sts.

Fasten off.

Elm Leaf Border

(Make 18 leaves in Yarn A and 14 in Yarn B.)
Make 4 leaves in Yarn A following the Elm Leaf instructions on page 212. For the remaining Elm leaves, use the Elm Leaf instructions on page 212, but attach the Border leaves together as you work as follows: At the beginning of Rows 4 and 6, instead of beginning the row with ch 3, work 3 sl sts in the edge of the same row on a finished leaf. Attach leaves together, alternating Yarn A and Yarn B, creating 2 9-leaf panels and 2 7-leaf panels.

Inner Border

RND 1: Using Yarn C, beginning with a Yarn A leaf next to a corner on a 9-leaf panel, sc in the base of the leaf, *ch 8, sc in base of next leaf; repeat from * until you have the 9 leaves joined in a row. Ch 10 for corner, sc in base of the next Yarn A leaf on a 7-leaf panel, **ch 8, sc in base of next leaf; repeat from ** until you have the 7 leaves joined in a row. Ch 10 for corner, sc in the base of the first Yarn A leaf on the remaining 9 leaf panel. Repeat from first * for the remaining 2 sides, ending with a sl st in the first sc.
RND 2: Ch 3, *dc in each st and ch along the side until you reach the 10-ch corner. Dc in first ch of corner, sk 8 ch, dc in last ch of corner; repeat from * around. Sl st in top of beg ch-3 to join.
Fasten off and weave in ends.

Grape Leaf

(Make 1 with Yarn D.)

Ch 15.

ROW 1: Sc in back half of 2nd ch from hook and next 12 ch, 5 sc in last ch, rotate work and sc in other half of next 10 ch. Turn—28 sts.

ROW 2: Ch 1, sk 1st st, sc in next 10 sts, 2 sc in next 3 sts, sc in next 10 sts. Turn—26 sts.

ROW 3: Ch 1, sk 1st st, sc in next 11 sts, 2 sc in next 3 sts, sc in next 9 sts. Turn.

ROW 4: Ch 1, sk 1st st, sc in next 10 sts, 2 sc in next 3 sts, sc in next 10 sts. Turn.

ROW 5: Ch 3, dc in next 12 sts, ch 1, sc in side of last dc, sc in next 2 sts, ch 3, dc in next 13 sts. Turn.

ROW 6: Ch 1, sk 1st st, sl st in next 4 sts, ch 4, tr in same st as last sl st, tr in next 2 sts, dc in next 6 sts, ch 1, work 3 sc along side of last dc and ch-3 of previous row, sc in next 4 sts, ch 3, dc in next 5 sts, tr in next 4 sts.

Fasten off.

Border Grape Leaf

(Make 4 with Yarn D.)

Work as for Grape Leaf, substituting Alternate Row 6.

ALTERNATE ROW 6: Cut working yarn to 1 yd. (.9m). Ch 1, sk
1st st, sl st in next 4 sts, ch 4, tr in same st as last sl st, tr in next
2 sts, dc in next 6 sts, sc in 3rd or 4th row of Elm Leaf next to
corner, work 3 sc along side of last dc and ch-3 of previous row
on Grape Leaf, ch 7, pass the working yarn through the ch-8
loop of dark green on Elm Border, sc in next 4 sts, ch 3, sl st in
3rd or 4th row of Elm Leaf on opposite side of corner, dc in
next 5 sts, tr in next 4 sts.
Fasten off.

Outer Border of Rug

RND 1: Attach Yarn C to the tip of any Elm Leaf. *Ch 8, sc in
next Elm Leaf; repeat from * along one side. After the last Elm
Leaf on a side, ch 15, tr in the side edge of the Grape Leaf, ch 8,
dc in tip of grape leaf, (ch 1, dc in tip of Grape Leaf) twice, ch
8, tr in side edge of Grape Leaf, ch 15, sc in first Elm Leaf of next
side. Repeat from first * for each side and corner, ending with a
sl st to join round.

RND 2: Ch 3, *dc in each st and chain to corner [ch-1 sp at tip
of Grape Leaf], (dc, ch 2, dc) in corner; repeat from * around,
dc to beg of rnd, join with sl st in top of beg ch-3.

RND 3: Rep Rnd 2 with Yarn F.

RND 4: Rep Rnd 2 with Yarn C.

Fasten off and weave in ends.

Ivy Leaf

(Make 2 using Yarn F.)

Ch 4.

ROW 1: 6 dc in 4th ch from hook. Turn—7 sts.

ROW 2: Ch 3, dc in next 3 sts, 2 dc in next st, dc in next 2 sts, 2 dc in top of ch-3. Turn—10 sts.

ROW 3: Ch 3, dc in next 4 sts, 3 dc in next st, dc in next 4 sts, 2 dc in top of ch-3. Turn—14 sts.

ROW 4: Ch 3, dc in next 6 sts, 2 dc in next 2 sts, dc in next 5 sts, dc in top of ch-3. Turn—17 sts.

ROW 5: Ch 3, dc in next 7 sts, 2 dc in next 2 sts, dc in next 7 sts, dc in top of ch-3. Turn—20 sts.

ROW 6: Ch 1, sk 1st st, sl st in next 5 sts, ch 3, dc in next 9 sts. Turn—10 sts.

ROW 7: Ch 3, sk 1st st, dc2tog, dc in next 4 sts, dc2tog. Turn—7 sts.

ROW 8: Ch 3, sk 1st st, dc2tog, dc in next st, dc2tog. Turn—4 sts.

ROW 9: Ch 2, sk 1st st, yo, pull up a loop in next st, yo, pull through 2 loops, yo, pull up a loop in top of ch-3, yo, pull through 2 loops, yo, pull through all loops on hook. Fasten off.

Oak Leaf

(Make 2 in Yarn E, 1 each in Yarns A, B, D, F and G.)

Ch 4.

ROW 1: Dc in 4th ch from hook. Turn—2 sts.

ROW 2: Ch 3, dc in next st. Turn—2 sts.

ROW 3: Ch 3, dc in next st, dc in top of ch-3. Turn—3 sts.

ROW 4: Ch 6, dc in 3rd ch from hook and next 3 ch, dc in next 2 sts, dc in top of ch-3. Turn—8 sts.

ROWS 5-9: Ch 5, dc in 3rd ch from hook and next 3 ch, dc in next 4 sts. Turn—9 sts.

ROW 10: Ch 3, dc in next 3 sts. Turn—4 sts.

ROW 11: Ch 2, sk 1st st, yo, pull up a loop in next st, yo, pull through 2 loops, yo, pull up a loop in top of ch-3, yo, pull through 2 loops, yo, pull through all loops on hook.

Eucalyptus Leaf

(Make 2 in Yarn H, 1 each in Yarns B, D, E and G.)

Ch 11.

ROW 1: Working in the back half of ea st, sl st in 2nd and 3rd chs from hook, sc in next 2 ch, hdc in next 2 ch, dc in next 3 ch, 10 tr in last ch, rotate work and dc in other half of next 3 ch, hdc in next 2 ch, sc in next ch, sl st in next ch.

Fasten off.

Maple Leaf

(Make 1 in Yarn A and 1 in Yarn B.)

Leaf Base

Ch 6.

ROW 1: 2 dc in 4th ch from hook, 3 dc in next ch, 2 dc in last ch. Turn—8 sts.

ROW 2: Ch 3, dc in next 3 sts, 3 dc in next st, dc in next 3 sts, dc in top of ch-3. Turn—11 sts.

ROW 3: Ch 3, dc in next 4 sts, 2 dc in next 2 sts, dc in next 4 sts, dc in top of ch-3. Turn—14 sts.

ROW 4: Ch 3, dc in next 6 sts, 2 dc in next 2 sts, dc in next 5 sts, dc in top of ch-3. Turn—17 sts.

ROW 5: Ch 3, dc in next 7 sts, 2 dc in next 2 sts, dc in next 7 sts, dc in top of ch-3. Turn—20 sts.

Do not break yarn.

Left Point

ROW 1: Continuing with the working yarn, ch 3, sk next st, dc in next 5 sts. Turn—6 sts.

ROW 2: Ch 3, sk 1st st, dc in next 3 sts, sk next st, dc in top of ch-3. Turn—5 sts.

ROW 3: Ch 3, sk 1st st, (yo, pull up a loop in next st, yo, pull through 2 loops) twice, yo, pull up a loop in top of ch-3, yo, pull through 2 loops, yo, pull through all loops on hook. Fasten off.

Center Point

Join a new length of yarn to the next free st on Row 5 of Leaf Base, next to the Left Point.

ROW 1: Ch 3, dc in next 7 sts. Turn—8 sts.

ROW 2: Ch 3, sk 1st st, dc in next 5 sts, sk next st, dc in top of ch-3. Turn—7 sts.

ROW 3: Ch 3, sk 1st st, dc in next 4 sts, sk next st, dc in top of ch-3. Turn—6 sts.

ROW 4: Ch 3, sk 1st st, dc in next 3 sts, sk next st, dc in top of ch-3. Turn—5 sts.

ROW 5: Ch 3, sk 1st st, (yo, pull up a loop in next st, yo, pull through 2 loops) twice, yo, pull up a loop in top of ch-3, yo, pull through 2 loops, yo, pull through all loops on hook. Fasten off.

Right Point

Join a new length of yarn to the next free st on Row 5 of Leaf Base, next to the Center Point.

ROW 1: Ch 3, dc in next 4 sts, dc in top of ch-3. Turn—6 sts.

ROW 2: Ch 3, sk 1st st, dc in next 3 sts, sk next st, dc in top of ch-3. Turn—5 sts.

ROW 3: Ch 3, sk 1st st, (yo, pull up a loop in next st, yo, pull through 2 loops) twice, yo, pull up a loop in top of ch-3, yo, pull through 2 loops, yo, pull through all loops on hook. Fasten off.

Rug Center

Once all of the leaves are crocheted, arrange them as shown below, or as you choose. Sew leaves together where they touch with yarn that matches at least 1 of the leaves, then sew the rug center to the inner edge of the inner border.

Fulling

Baste the finished rug to the nylon netting with the pearl cotton. Tightly roll the rug up into a log shape, pull the nylon stocking over it and tie closed. Turn on the dryer to preheat it. Wet the bundle thoroughly with warm water. Squeeze out the excess. Put the rug in the dryer with tennis balls for agitation. Check every 10 minutes to see if piece is fulled. When the rug is completely fulled, remove the basting and netting. Squeeze out excess water. Pull to shape and let it dry flat.

Multi-Technique Projects

One of the most rewarding results of trying out different techniques is when you get to combine them to make a special project. This section combines techniques from the previous chapters, building projects that incorporate several felting processes. Be sure to go back and read the previous chapters if you need a refresher on any of the techniques.

Poinsettia Mat

This project is quick and easy to knit and the knitted fabric provides the perfect background for needle felting. The poinsettias can be worked in the traditional red and white, or you can add other colors to liven it up.

The project shown at left was made using Dale of Norway Falk (100% wool, 1¾ oz./50g, 116yds/106m) in color 7562 and Harrisville Designs Fleece in the following colors: 002 Red and 044 White.

SKILL LEVEL

Beginner

FINISHED SIZE

8" × 8" (20cm × 20cm)

YARN

1 (1¾ oz./50g, 116yds/106m) skein worsted weight yarn

KNITTING NEEDLES

Size 6 (4mm) straight knitting needles

NOTIONS

Tapestry needle

GAUGE

14 sts and 16 rows = 4" (10cm) in St st

FELTING SUPPLIES

Small amounts of feltable wool fiber in several colors for embellishments

Size 36 felting needles

Felting needle holder

Felting mat

Pattern transfer supplies

1 Knit base

CO 40 sts.

ROW 1: (K1, p1) rep across.

ROW 2: (P1, k1) rep across.

Repeat Rows 1–2 once.

ROW 5: (K1, p1) twice, k to the last 4 sts, (k1, p1) twice.

ROW 6: (P1, k1) twice, p to the last 4 sts, (p1, k1) twice.

Repeat Rows 5–6 24 times.

Repeat Rows 1–2 twice.

BO, weave in ends.

2 Needle felting

Lay the outline of the larger leaves over the knitting, using the pattern as a guide for placement (see page 227). Place the felting mat under the knitting. As you needle felt, move the mat often to keep it under the section you are working and to keep the fibers from sticking into the mat. Begin needling the outlines of the design in place, then fill in the shapes. Add depth with shading. Repeat for the smaller leaves, overlapping the larger leaves. Attach embellishments as desired.

Pattern shown at actual size.

Oak Leaves Wall Banner

This easy-to-knit banner is a great little project that allows you to try many aspects of felting, from shading and three-dimensional forms in needle felting, to combining wet felting with needle felting. By changing the colors of the leaves, or by using holly or a spring flower instead of leaves, you can make a banner for each season of the year.

The project shown at left was made using Brown Sheep Company Lamb's Pride Bulky (85% wool, 15% mohair, 4 oz./113g, 125 yd./114m) color M115 Oatmeal and Louet fiber pack #2.

SKILL LEVEL

Beginner

FINISHED SIZE

10¾" × 6" (27cm × 15cm)

YARN

1 (4 oz./113g, 125 yd./114m) skein bulky weight yarn

KNITTING NEEDLES

Size 10½ (6.5mm) straight knitting needles

NOTIONS

Tapestry needle
7" (18cm) length of ¼" (6mm) dowel rod
2 wooden stoppers
12" (30cm) length of ribbon

GAUGE

14 sts and 20 rows = 4" (10cm) in St st

FELTING SUPPLIES

Small amounts of feltable wool fiber in several colors for embellishments
Size 36 felting needle
Felting mat
Pattern transfer supplies
Warm, soapy water
Cool water for rinsing

1 **Knit base**
CO 1 st.
ROW 1: Kfb—2 sts.
ROW 2: Pfb, p1—3 sts.
ROW 3: Kfb, k2—4 sts.
ROW 4: Pfb, p3—5 sts.
ROW 5: Kfb, k rem sts—6 sts.
ROW 6: Pfb, p rem sts—7 sts.
Rep Rows 5–6 7 times—21 sts.
NEXT ROW: K all sts.
NEXT ROW: K2, p to last two sts, k2.
Repeat last 2 rows until banner
measures 9" (23cm) from point.
NEXT ROW (RS): (K2tog, yo) 10
times, k1.
BO.

2 **Transfer design**
Enlarge the pattern to the
recommended size (see page
231). Transfer the pattern to the banner
(see *Transferring Patterns*, page 107). Lay
the leaves over the knitting, using the
pattern on the opposite page as a guide
for placement. Place the felting mat
under the knitting. As you needle felt,
move the mat often to keep it under
the section you are working and to
keep the fibers from sticking to the mat.
Begin needling the outlines of the leaves
in place, then fill in the shapes. Add
details, such as veins, and shading with
additional colors of fiber.

3 Create acorns

To make the hanging acorn, wet felt a 2g ball of fiber into an acorn shape by first working it into a 1" (3cm) ball, then pressing the sides and one end into an acorn shape (see *Dimensional Felting*, page 48). Allow the wool to dry completely. After the wool is dry, needle felt a small amount of wool to the acorn to add shading. Then needle felt fiber onto the top of the form to represent the cap of the acorn, tucking the edges of the fiber under to create the cap shape. Stitch the acorn to the bottom point of the banner. Create 2 more acorns in the same manner using 1g of fiber each and shaping them to have flat backs. Needle felt the smaller acorns to the banner.

Thread the dowel through the holes at the top of the banner and add a wooden stopper to each end of the dowel. Tie the ribbon to the ends of the dowel for hanging.

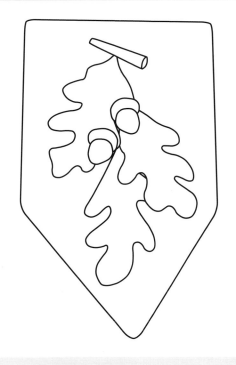

Enlarge to 300% to bring to full size.

Meandering Leaves Container

This simple needle-felted design can be worked on any surface from fabric to knitted, woven, or crocheted projects. This easy-to-make container is just one example of what you can embellish with these lovely leaves.

The project shown at left was made using Kraemer Yarns Naturally Nazareth (100% wool, 3½ oz./100g, 184 yd./168m) color Spring and Harrisville Designs Fleece in color 044 White.

SKILL LEVEL

Beginner

FINISHED SIZE

Approximately 4" (10cm) across and 6" (15cm) tall, after fulling

YARN

1 (3½ oz./100g, 184 yd./168m) skein feltable worsted weight yarn

HOOK

US H (5mm) crochet hook

NOTIONS

Tapestry needle
Pearl cotton
Removable marker

GAUGE

16½ hdc and 12 rows = 4" (10cm), before fulling

FULLING SUPPLIES

Washing machine
Dishwashing soap

FELTING SUPPLIES

2g feltable wool fiber
Size 36 felting needle
Felting mat
Pattern transfer supplies

1 Crochet container

Ch 3.

RND 1: 6 hdc in 3rd ch from hook. Do not turn.

RND 2: Continuing in the round, work 2 hdc in each st around, pm in last st—12 sts.

RND 3: (Hdc in next st, 2 dc in next st) 6 times, move marker to last st—18 sts.

RND 4: (Hdc in next 2 sts, 2 hdc in next st) 6 times, move marker to last st—24 sts.

RND 5: (Hdc in next 3 sts, 2 hdc in next st) 6 times, move marker to last st—30 sts.

RND 6: (Hdc in next 4 sts, 2 hdc in next st) 6 times, move marker to last st—36 sts.

Cont as set, working incs at 6 points every rnd, until you have 78 sts—13 rnds total.

Work even in hdc for 7 (18cm).

Fasten off and weave in ends.

2 Full container

Baste the opening closed with pearl cotton. Throw it in the washer on the hot/cold setting and the lowest water level with a bit of dishwashing soap. Check every 5–10 minutes to see if the fulling process is complete. When the container is fulled, remove the pearl cotton, shape the container, and let dry.

3
Needle felt design
Transfer the pattern below to the container (see *Transferring Patterns*, page 107). Place the felting mat inside the container. As you needle felt, move the mat often to keep it under the section you are working on and to keep the fibers from sticking into the mat. Begin needling the outlines of the design in place, then fill in the shapes.

Pattern shown at actual size.

Ocean in a Basket

When researching hat making for this book, I discovered the wonders of water-based shellac. I was curious whether it could be used in other felting projects, namely my flimsy felted bowls and baskets. This crocheted basket is the result, combining crochet, a wet-felted lining and needle-felted embellishments, stiffened with water-based shellac.

The project shown at left was made using Kraemer Yarns Bear Creek (99% wool, 1% nylon, 7 oz./200g,130 yd./119m), color Kiwi Ice and Harrisville Designs Fleece in the following colors: 010 Spruce (A), 031 Cobalt (B), 021 Violet, 037 Cocoa, 044 White, 042 Camel and 041 Sandlewood.

SKILL LEVEL

Intermediate

FINISHED SIZE

Approximately 11" (28cm) across at widest point, 6" (15cm) tall, with 7" (18cm) base, after fulling

YARN

1 (7 oz./200g,130 yd./119m) skein of feltable super bulky weight yarn

HOOK

US N (10mm) crochet hook

NOTIONS

Tapestry needle
Removable marker

GAUGE

6 dc and 4 rows = 4" (10cm) after fulling

FELTING SUPPLIES

5 oz. (141g) feltable wool fiber in 2 colors, 4 oz. (113g) of Fiber A and 1 oz. (28g) of Fiber B
Small amounts of feltable wool fiber in several colors for embellishments
Size 36 felting needle
Felting mat
Water-based shellac
Small plastic trash bag
Warm, soapy water
Dowel rod
Cool water for rinsing

1 Crochet basket

Ch 4.

RND 1: 11 dc in 4th ch from hook, join with sl st in top of ch-4. Do not turn—12 sts.

RND 2: Cont in the round, ch 3, (dc in next st, 2 dc in next st) 6 times, join with sl st in top of beg ch-3, place marker in last st—18 sts.

RND 3: Ch 3, (dc in next 2 sts, 2 dc in next st) 6 times, move marker to last st, join with sl st in top of beg ch-3—24 sts.

RND 4: Ch 3, (dc in next 3 sts, 2 dc in next st) 6 times, move marker to last st, join with sl st in top of beg ch-3—30 sts.

RND 5: Ch 3, (dc in next 4 sts, 2 dc in next st) 6 times, move marker to last st, join with sl st in top of beg ch-3—36 sts.

RND 6: Ch 3, (dc in next 5 sts, 2 dc in next st) 6 times, move marker to last st, join with sl st in top of beg ch-3—42 sts.

Work even in dc for 7 (18cm).

Fasten off and weave in ends.

2 Add lining

Lay down a 2" (5cm) thick layer of Fiber A inside the crocheted basket. Lay 3"–5" (8cm–13cm) strips of Fiber B over the edges of the basket, on top of the layer of Fiber A. Place the plastic trash bag inside the basket. Wet the basket and fiber with warm, soapy water. Massage the fiber and basket, pressing the water into both, from the inside and outside, until the fiber begins to felt to the basket. Check the basket often to make sure that the fibers are distributed as you desire. Keeping the plastic bag in the basket, fold the basket in half and felt it (see *Flat Felting, Step by Step*, pages 42-47). Rinse the basket in cool water, pull roughly into desired shape, and let it dry.

3 Needle felt embellishments

When the basket is completely dry, hold it up to the light and check for thin areas or any places where the lining may not have felted to the crochet. Fill in any thin areas with small tufts of green lining and needle felt in place. Needle felt any loose sections of lining to the crochet.

Turn the basket inside out and transfer the pattern to the inside of the basket (see *Transferring Patterns*, page 107). Needle felt the outline of each part of the pattern. Continue needle felting the design, filling in each portion, then add shading with color.

When you are satisfied with the basket, mix the water-based shellac following the manufacturer's instructions, coat the inside of the basket, form it into the shape you desire and allow it to dry completely.

Enlarge to 200% to bring to full size.

Friendly Wizard

For a fantasy and sorcery fan, this is just the project to add a little magic to your fiber work. This project combines needle felting and wet felting to create a wise, old wizard, who can easily be adapted to resemble characters from your favorite books or movies.

The project shown at left was made using Harrisville Designs Fleece in the following colors: 044 White (A), 042 Camel (B), 031 Cobalt (C), 033 Midnight Blue (D), 021 Violet (E), 008 Hemlock (F) and 010 Spruce (G).

SKILL LEVEL

Intermediate

FINISHED SIZE

15½" × 6" × 4½"
(39cm × 15cm × 11cm)

MATERIALS

2¾ oz. (77g) feltable wool fiber in 7 colors, ¾ oz. (20g) of Fiber A, ¼ oz. (7g) of Fiber B, ¾ oz. (20g) of Fiber C, ⅓ oz. (10g) each of Fibers D, E and F, and 2g Fiber G

Small amounts of feltable wool fiber in several colors for embellishments

1 oz. (28g) uncarded longwool locks

1 sheet of prefelt

Size 36 and 40 felting needles

Felting needle holder

Felting mat

Toothpick

Bubble wrap

Netting (optional)

Warm, soapy water

Dowel rod

Rubberbands

Cool water for rinsing

Steam iron (optional)

1 Make head

Create a basic head sculpture using Fiber A as the base and Fiber B as the skintone of your choice (see *Step-by-Step Faces*, pages 116-120).

Using approximately ¼ oz. (7g) of Fiber C, form a cone shape on top of the head for a hat that is approximately 3½" × 2½" (9cm × 6cm) after needle felting. Embellish the hat with a swirl of Fiber D.

Separate the longwool locks and attach the remaining locks around the head, just below the hat and around the face for the beard.

2 Make body

Needle felt the remainder of Fiber A into a 9" (23cm) tall cone that is 1½" (4cm) wide at the top and 4" (10cm) wide at the bottom. Completely cover the cone in Fiber C and needle felt in place. Separate Fiber G into 2 1g pieces. Needle felt these pieces into pointed shoes and attach them to the bottom of the cone.

To form the 1st arm, needle felt 4g of Fiber C into a cylinder approximately 1" × 6" (3cm × 15cm). Repeat for a second arm. To make the hands, use 1g of Fiber B for each hand. Make the fingers and thumbs by rolling a small cylinder of wool with a toothpick, then needle felt. Needle felt the remaining portion of the wool to make a small, flat dome shape for the palm and attach the fingers and thumbs. Attach a hand to the end of each arm. Needle felt the arms to attach them to the body.

3 Make coat

Using the pattern below, cut the prefelt into stars and moons, making 10–15 pieces. Lay out Fibers C, D, E and F on the bubble wrap, covering a 12" × 18" (30cm × 46cm) area. Scatter stars and moons randomly over the batt. Felt the batt (see *Flat Felting, Step by Step* pages 42-47). Lay flat to dry. Iron to flatten further if needed.

Cut a 3" × 12" (8cm × 30cm) strip from the felted batt. Cut this strip into 2 3" × 6" (8cm × 15cm) pieces, and sew each piece into a cylinder for sleeves. Cut slits in the remaining batt for sleeve openings. Wrap the batt around the wizard, placing the arms through the slits in the batt. Slide the sleeves over the arms and needle felt in place. Tie the coat closed with a sash.

Embellish the wizard with your choice of accessories.

Enlarge to 150% to bring to full size.

Glossary

Batt: A flat, rectangular sheet of fiber that has been cleaned and removed from a carding machine.

Blocking: Pulling and shaping a piece of work into its final form.

Drum carder: A machine with two drums that are covered with wire-studded cloth arranged in a frame with a crank handle or electric pulley system so that the two drums rotate to card fibers.

Felt: Fibers that have matted together.

Felting: The process of causing fibers to mat together.

Felting needle: A barbed needle used for forcing fibers to mat together.

Fulling: The process of causing fabric, such as knitted, crocheted or woven fabrics, to shrink and condense.

Hand card: A comb that resembles a large cat or dog brush. It is a rectangle of wood covered on one side with wire needles that are bent toward a handle. Carders come in pairs to brush against each other to blend and straighten fibers.

Hardening: Compressing fibers with pressure.

Hat blocks: Wood forms carved into hat shapes.

Hat forms: Plastic forms molded into hat shapes.

Laminated: In felting, fibers that are felted to a fabric. Also called Nuno felting.

Micron: A unit of measurement for measuring wool fibers. One micron is a millionth of a meter.

Nuno: A felting technique in which fibers are felted to a fabric.

Pencil roving: A length of roving that is about ½" (1cm) thick.

Pinch test: Pinching a small section of fibers and pulling slightly to see if the fibers have felted enough to hold together.

Prefelt: Fibers that have tangled together enough to become a fragile fabric, but have not felted completely.

Rolag: A thick rope of carded fiber that has been rolled off a carding machine; a woolen fiber preparation.

Roving: A thick rope of combed fiber that has been pulled off a carding machine in strips so that it is still aligned in a worsted form.

Shaping: Pulling, pushing and pinning to create the finished shape of the project.

Sliver: A combed rope of worsted fibers.

Top: See *sliver*.

Woolen: Fibers that have been cleaned and carded, but the fibers are long and short and are jumbled rather than lying parallel to each other.

Worsted: Fibers that have been cleaned and combed, which removes the shorter fibers and positions the long remaining fibers so that they are parallel to each other.

Abbreviations

Knitting

beg - begin, beginning
BO - bind off
CO - cast on
cont - continue, continuing
dec - decrease
dpn(s) - double pointed needle(s)
ea - each
est - established
foll - follow, following
inc - increase
k - knit
k2tog - knit two together as one
k3tog - knit three together as one
kfb - knit into the front and back of the stitch
kwise - knitwise, as if to knit
m - marker

p - purl
p2tog - purl two stitches together as one
patt - pattern
pfb - purl into the front and back of the stitch
pm - place marker
rem - remain, remaining
rep - repeat
rnd(s) - round, rounds
RS - right side
sl - slip
sm - slip marker
st(s) - stitch, stitches
St st - Stockinette stitch
tbl - through back loop
WS - wrong side
yo - yarn over

Crochet

beg - begin, beginning
ch - chain
ch-sp - chain space
dc - double crochet
dec - decrease
ea - each
hdc - half double crochet
hk - hook

lp(s) - loop, loops
patt - pattern
pm - place marker
rep(s) - repeat, repeats
sc - single crochet
sk - skip
st(s) - stitch, stitches
tr - triple crochet

Yarn Weight Guidelines

Since the names given to different weights of yarn can vary widely depending on the country of origin or the yarn manufacturer's preference, The Craft Yarn Council of America has put together a standard yarn weight system. Look for a picture of a skein of yarn with a number 0–6 on most kinds of yarn to figure out its "official" weight. Gauge is given over 4" (10cm) of Stockinette stitch. The information in the chart below is taken from www.yarnstandards.com.

YARN WEIGHT SYMBOL & CATEGORY NAMES	0 LACE	1 SUPER FINE	2 FINE	3 LIGHT	4 MEDIUM	5 BULKY	6 SUPER BULKY
Type of Yarns in Category	Fingering 10-count crochet thread	Sock, Fingering, Baby	Sport, Baby	DK, Light Worsted	Worsted, Afghan, Aran	Chunky, Craft, Rug	Bulky, Roving
Knit Gauge Range* in Stockinette Stitch to 4 inches	33–40** sts	27–32 sts	23–26 sts	21–24 st	16–20 sts	12–15 sts	6–11 sts
Recommended Needle in Metric Size Range	1.5–2.25 mm	2.25—3.25 mm	3.25—3.75 mm	3.75—4.5 mm	4.5—5.5 mm	5.5—8 mm	8 mm and larger
Recommended Needle U.S. Size Range	000–1	1 to 3	3 to 5	5 to 7	7 to 9	9 to 11	11 and larger
Crochet Gauge* Ranges in Single Crochet to 4 inch	32–42 double crochets**	21–32 sts	16–20 sts	12–17 sts	11–14 sts	8–11 sts	5–9 sts
Recommended Hook in Metric Size Range	Steel*** 1.6–1.4 mm	2.25—3.5 mm	3.5—4.5 mm	4.5—5.5 mm	5.5—6.5 mm	6.5—9 mm	9 mm and larger
Recommended Hook U.S. Size Range	Steel*** 6, 7, 8 Regular hook B–1	B–1 to E–4	E–4 to 7	7 to I–9	I–9 to K–10 1/2	K–10 1/2 to M–13	M–13 and larger

* GUIDELINES ONLY: The above reflect the most commonly used gauges and needle or hook sizes for specific yarn categories.

** Lace weight yarns are usually knitted or crocheted on larger needles and hooks to create lacy, openwork patterns. Accordingly, a gauge range is difficult to determine. Always follow the gauge stated in your pattern.

*** Steel crochet hooks are sized differently from regular hooks—the higher the number, the smaller the hook, which is the reverse of regular hook sizing.

Knitting Needle Conversions

DIAMETER (MM)	US SIZE
2	0
2.25	1
2.75	2
3.25	3
3.5	4
3.75	5
4	6
4.5	7
5	8
5.5	9
6	10
6.5	10½
8	11
9	13
10	15
12.75	17
15	19
20	36

Crochet Hook Conversions

DIAMETER (MM)	US SIZE
2.25	B/1
2.75	C/2
3.25	D/3
3.5	E/4
3.75	F/5
4	G/6
5	H/8
5.5	I/9
6	J/10
6.5	K/10½
8	L/11
9	M/13
10	N/15

Metric Conversion Chart

TO CONVERT	TO	MULTIPLY BY
Inches	Centimeters	2.54
Centimeters	Inches	0.4
Feet	Centimeters	30.5
Centimeters	Feet	0.03
Yards	Meters	0.9
Meters	Yards	1.1
Sq. Inches	Sq. Centimeters	6.45
Sq. Centimeters	Sq. Inches	0.16
Sq. Feet	Sq. Meters	0.09
Sq. Meters	Sq. Feet	10.8
Sq. Yards	Sq. Meters	0.8
Sq. Meters	Sq. Yards	1.2
Pounds	Kilograms	0.45
Kilograms	Pounds	2.2
Ounces	Grams	28.3
Grams	Ounces	0.035

Resources

You only have to search online under *feltmaking, felt artists* or *felting* to find locations of a variety of felting sites, from artist's individual sites to shops with felting supplies to felting associations. Following are some of my favorite sites for felting supplies and inspiration.

Fibers and Yarns

Araucania
www.araucaniayarns.com

Brown Sheep
www.brownsheep.com

Cascade
www.cascadeyarns.com

Cranberry Moon Farm
www.goodwool.com

Dale of Norway
www.dale.no

Harrisville Designs
www.harrisville.com

Kraemer Yarns
www.kraemeryarns.com

Lorna's Laces
www.lornaslaces.net

Louet
www.louet.com

Marr Haven
www.marrhaven.com

Mountain Colors
www.mountaincolors.com

Noro
www.noroyarns.com

Hat-Making Supplies

Hat Shapers
www.hatshapers.com

Hooked on Felt
www.hookedonfelt.com

Judith M Hats & Millinery Supplies
www.judithm.com

American Felt Web Sites

North American Felters' Network (NAFN)
www.peak.org/%7Espark/feltmakers.html

The Northeast Feltmakers Guild (NFG)
www.northeastfeltmakersguild.org

International Felt Web Sites

Canberra Region Feltmakers
http://crfelters.org.au

GRIMA (Danish Feltmaker's Association)
www.grima.dk

International Feltmakers Association
www.feltmakers.com

Index

Discover More Ideas for Felting Fun

Felted Crochet

Jane Davis

This resource provides step-by-step instructions for easily creating 30 beautiful accents for home and wardrobe, including purses, bags, blankets, vest, pillows and more.

ISBN 10: 0-87349-887-9
ISBN 13: 978-0-87349-887-6
paperback
8¼" × 10⅞"
128 pages
FELCR

Knit Ponchos, Wraps & Scarves
Create 40 Quick and Contemporary Accessories

Jane Davis

Answering the demand for new scarf, poncho and shawl ideas, this book provides 40+ fun, contemporary projects knitters can create quickly and easily, many featuring popular novelty yarns. Includes projects for all skill levels.

ISBN 10: 0-87349-965-4
ISBN 13: 978-0-87349-965-1
paperback
8¼" × 10⅞"
128 pages
SCVSH

Bead Embroidery The Complete Guide
Bring New Dimension to Classic Needlework

Jane Davis

Discover how to transform your favorite projects into extraordinary artwork by fusing the crafts of embroidery and beading. This guide demonstrates how to create 20 beautiful projects.

ISBN 10: 0-87349-888-7
ISBN 13: 978-0-87349-888-3
hardcover with concealed spiral
5⅝" × 7⅝
256 pages"
BDEM

Needle Felting by Hand or Machine
15 Projects Using Easy-to-Learn Techniques

Linda Griepentrog and Pauline Richards

Tap into one of the hottest trends with this practical, full-color needle felting how-to. Create items for the home, wardrobe or to give as gifts.

ISBN 10: 0-89689-485-1
ISBN 13: 978-0-89689-485-3
paperback
8¼" × 10⅞"
128 pages
Z0749

Fabulous Felt
Over 30 Exquisite Ideas for Sophisticated Home Décor and Stunning Accessories

Sophie Bester

Combines felt with other popular crafts including beading, embroidery and appliqué. Features 32 stunning projects including photo frames, photo album covers, cushions, rugs, holiday decorations and children's gifts.

ISBN 10: 0-7153-2646-5
ISBN 13: 978-0-7153-2646-6
paperback
8" × 10"
120 pages
Z0865

Looking for more great craft ideas
Visit **www.mycraftivity.com**.
Connect. Create. Explore.